What Don't You Know?

Also available from Continuum:

Great Thinkers A–Z, edited by Julian Baggini and
Jeremy Stangroom

What Philosophers Think, edited by Julian Baggini and
Jeremy Stangroom

What More Philosophers Think, edited by Julian Baggini and
Jeremy Stangroom

What We Can Never Know, David Gamez

The Twenty Greatest Philosophy Books, James Garvey

How to Win Every Argument, Madsen Pirie

What Don't You Know?
Philosophical Provocations

Michael C. LaBossiere

continuum

Continuum

Continuum International Publishing Group
The Tower Building   80 Maiden Lane
11 York Road   Suite 704
London SE1 7NX   New York NY 10038
www.continuumbooks.com

First published 2008

British Library Cataloguing-in-Publication Data
A catalogue record for this book is available from the British Library.

ISBN: HB: 0-8264-9983-X
        978-0-8264-9983-7

        PB: 0-8264-9984-8
        978-0-8264-9984-4

Library of Congress Cataloging-in-Publication Data
A catalog record of this book is available from the Library of Congress.

Typeset by Servis Filmsetting Limited, Manchester
Printed and bound in Great Britain by MPG Books Ltd, Bodmin, Cornwall

Contents

Introduction

Welcome to *What Don't You Know?* In this work you will find a series of short, interesting and provocative discussions of controversial issues from a philosophical perspective.

This book is a collection of my writings for *The Philosophers' Magazine*. This magazine, created by Julian Baggini and Jeremey Stangroom, is devoted to presenting thought-provoking thoughts to the world. Since the world seems rather provoked, the magazine clearly has been a smashing success.

The story of this book begins in 1997 when I was asked to write an article for the magazine. The article had to be on something relevant to philosophy and needed to be neither too technical nor too boring. If you are familiar with contemporary philosophy, then you will have some idea of the challenge I faced. Fortunately, I was up to the challenge (or there was just enough unfilled space in the magazine) and the article was published.

After I had written a few more articles, Julian realized what many people already knew: in addition to being a running fanatic, I have a special gift for provoking people. He suggested that I take this talent and turn it loose on the world where it could do more damage . . . err . . . good. Thus, the philosophical provocations column was born. Since then, the column has appeared in each issue of the *Philosophers' Magazine* and each month on the magazine's website.

Realizing that all this writing amounted to enough material for a book, I decided to take the obvious logical step and assembled the diverse articles and columns into a more organized form. Of course, this assemblage would need a title.

Being a fan of Clint Eastwood's classic *A Fistful of Dollars*, I was originally inspired to call this book *A Fistful of Provocations.* This way, I could call the second book in the series *A Few Provocations More.* The third book would, naturally enough, be *The Good, the Bad and the Philosophical.*

Of course, as was pointed out to me, *A Fistful of Provocations* would be a somewhat confusing title for a philosophy book. People might not realize it was a philosophy book and could mistake it for a book on how to start bar fights. To avoid such misunderstandings, the book now bears the same subtitle as the column. This title is accurate, concise and something no one would associate with bar fights.

With the title done, the next step was to organize the work. After careful thought, I decided to divide the book into two main sections. The first section, 'Metaphysics and Epistemology: What there is and what you (don't) know about it', deals with (amazingly enough) both metaphysics and epistemology.

Metaphysics is a branch of philosophy concerned with the nature of reality. The existence of God, the nature of the human mind, and the nature of space-time are just a few of the matters that metaphysicians try to explain and analyse.

One sub-category of metaphysics is ontology ('the study of things') which aims at determining the contents of reality and in what relationships these things stand to each other. I mention this because I am an ontologist. Yes, some people have confused that with being a proctologist.

In popular usage, metaphysics now often refers to what lies beyond the physical realm. It is also often seen as being concerned with such things as psychic powers, spirits and magical crystals. However, this is quite distinct from philosophical metaphysics. Which is why, for example, when people ask me about the best sort of healing crystals to buy I have to say 'That's not the sort of metaphysics I do . . .' followed by 'OK, you want the pink rhomboid ones . . . they work best when inserted in your nose.'

Interestingly enough, what is now called 'metaphysics' was originally known as 'first philosophy'. The term 'metaphysics' arose from something of an accident and really has nothing to do with being about things beyond the physical.

According to the accepted tale, an editor of Aristotle's works put his writings on first philosophy right after his writings on physics. In a fit of originality, the editor called the writings on first philosophy 'the books that are after the books on physics'. Latin scholars later mistranslated this as 'the science of what is beyond physics'. Given this error, it is a good thing that the works on first philosophy were not placed after Aristotle's cookbook. If that had happened, people would be talking about metacooking and meta-cooking stores would no doubt be selling spiritual pies and books on the healing powers of saucepans. Of course, we will never know for sure what might have happened, which leads to the field of epistemology.

Epistemology is the study of knowledge. This branch of philoso-phy is focused on determining the possibility, nature and limits of knowledge. Epistemologists, philosophers who do epistemology, try to determine what knowledge might be and usually attempt to address the challenge put forth by sceptics who argue that we cannot know anything. While many people regard epistemology as rather boring, films such as *The Matrix* have helped make it much more interesting. This indicates that almost any academic subject can be improved by adding explosions and guns, lots of guns.

The second part of the book, 'Value: Ethics and Political and Social Thought – Good, Evil, Politics and All that Stuff', focuses on the value area of philosophy. This area is all about normative matters. Normative matters are those that involve judgements of worth and include such fields as law, ethics, aesthetics, religion and etiquette.

Ethics is perhaps the best-known value branch and addresses questions about how we are to live and what we should and should not do. Naturally, it also deals with good, evil and all that stuff. Not surprisingly, this area is highly relevant to life and includes some of the great controversies that people face such as the debates over abor-tion, stem cell research, and war.

Aesthetics is the branch of philosophy concerned with theories of art and beauty. Problems in this area deal with such matters as the nature of beauty, arguments about censorship, and concerns about the rights of artists.

The sub-section on political and social thought is rather self-explanatory: thoughts on politics and social matters. This is a rather broad area as it deals with almost anything relating to social and political matters. Naturally, I fully exploited this broadness and wrote about whatever subject happened to provoke me at the time.

Now, let the provoking begin.

PART ONE:

METAPHYSICS AND EPISTEMOLOGY:

*WHAT THERE IS AND WHAT YOU
(DON'T) KNOW ABOUT IT*

1   The Mind

While most people assume they have minds (and entertain some doubts about others, especially reality TV show stars), there are many questions about the nature of the mind. In fact, there is some question about whether there are such things. This subsection includes provocations written specifically about the mind and what it might or might not be. Also included is a discussion of one of my favourite topics, ghosts.

A mind for all reasons

While the debate over the mind has persisted for centuries, the latest round pits the scientific materialists against what has been called the commonsense view of the mind.

The materialists contend the mind is the brain (or its functions) and deny the existence of an immaterial mind. The commonsense view is that while the brain has an important role in mental matters, the true person is an immaterial entity.

While the evidence for scientific materialism seems overwhelming (at least to its proponents), many still hold the commonsense view and some express serious concerns about the implications of materialism. In order to change these minds, the defenders of materialism use of a variety of stock arguments, some of which will now be considered.

One method begins by presenting cases in which the errors of common sense are exposed and corrected by science. One popular example is how science showed that viruses and bacteria, not witches and demons, cause disease. Another is that science replaced the mistaken view that the sun sets with the correct view that the earth rotates us away from the sun. Given the general unreliability of common sense, the argument proceeds, there is every reason to believe it is mistaken about the mind. Hence, the materialist view should be accepted.

One reply is that even though some commonsense beliefs turned out to be false, common sense is generally reliable. After all, if most people got things wrong most of the time, we would expect a great deal more trouble than we actually have. Further, while there have been clear failures of common sense, there are many more cases in which it is correct. For example, it is common sense that wood burns, ice cools, sharp things can kill, food and drink are needed for life, and so on. Finally, science has had its share of serious failures and errors as well. Thus, it would seem that this method is hardly conclusive.

A second stock method focuses on explaining the widespread belief in the immaterial mind. Not surprisingly, proponents of common sense note that a reasonable way to explain this belief is that the mind is immaterial. To use an analogy, one reasonable way to explain the widespread belief in trees is that trees exist.

Naturally, the materialists must provide an alternative explanation which does not involve the existence of such minds. Driving a road long ago paved by Immanuel Kant,[1] psychologist Paul Bloom[2] contends that the mind–body distinction is an inherent part of thought. As Kant claimed, although we have no proper evidence for a metaphysical self, we cannot help but believe in it. Until, the materialist would add, science sets us straight: we believe in it not because it exists, but because of the nature of the (material) mind. Thus, the belief is accounted for without the existence of immaterial minds.

While seemingly reasonable, this approach is not without peril: if one intrinsic part of thought is in error, then there is a good possibility that there are other defects in the machinery. The possibility of such defects provides good grounds for being sceptical about human reason – including that used in science. Thus, given this alleged defect in the mind, it seems prudent to take a sceptical approach to materialism as well.

One major obstacle the materialists face is the concern that materialism is a threat to morality. One reply is that, for example, it was feared that the heliocentric view and its accompanying materialism would have dire consequences for morality (and religion). It turned out the worry was groundless. So, there is no need to be worried about a materialistic view of the mind being a threat to morality.

In reply, it does seem that the materialist view of the outer world has had some rather serious moral consequences. As various thinkers have argued, as the material and mechanistic view of the outer world developed, so too did the tendency to regard the world as a mere commodity – something to be used and exploited. It seems likely that the same would also be true of the inner world: the more people regard other people as mere material mechanisms, the more likely it is that they will regard them as things to be used and exploited. Thus, there does seem to be something to be worried about – the last thing we need is another reason to treat people worse than we already do.

Cloning and the mind

The notion that beings have minds distinct from their bodies has largely fallen out of favour. Advancements in biology, genetics and neurophysiology seem to have left no place for the mind. Instead, what was called the mind is now explained in terms of the nervous system, behavioural conditioning and genetics. Ironically, recent findings in the field of cloning suggest that the mind might exist.

In science fiction, clones are often presented as exact duplicates of the original, with the same physical and mental traits. Popular sentiment also seems to hold such a view and even thinkers such as Jeremy Rifkin[3] seem to regard cloning as making 'a Xerox' of the original.

However, recent studies of cloned animals reveal that current cloning techniques produce animals that are as distinct in their personalities as animals produced by 'natural' means of reproduction. Texas A&M, which has been on the forefront of animal cloning, has found that cloned pigs differ from each other in, among other things, their food preferences and degree of friendliness towards human beings. Their cloned cat, Cc (Carbon Copy)[4] is both more curious and more playful than the 'original' cat, Rainbow.

While no artificial human clones are known to exist, 'natural' clones do – identical twins. While such twins are genetically the same and typically brought up in the same conditions, they often have very different personalities.

Given that the clones are genetically the same and are typically raised in similar environments, it seems reasonable to consider the possibility of a non-physical factor that causes the difference in personality. After all, once the physical factors are accounted for, what would seem to remain would be the non-physical. In light of the history of philosophy, the most plausible candidate would be the mind.

Following thinkers such as Descartes,[5] the mind is a conscious, thinking thing which makes each thinking entity the entity it is, distinct from all other things. Presumably, the mind is also the seat of the personality and contains the qualities that are manifested as personality traits, such as the being's friendliness or curiosity.

Not surprisingly, thinkers disagree about the nature of such a mind. Descartes regarded it as an immaterial substance, Locke[6] regarded it as consciousness (apparently connected to the soul), and Hume[7] regarded it as a bundle of perceptions. More recent philosophers have taken the mind to be a set of non-physical qualities (but not a substance) and others regard it as a set of functions. Fortunately, it is sufficient for this discussion to regard the mind, whatever it might precisely be, as distinct from the physical makeup of the organism.

Such a mind would explain the difference in personality between twins and clones. Although the body has been cloned, the mind has not. Thus, each organism has its own, unique mind and hence its own distinct personality and identity.

Despite the appeal of the mind, fairness and good philosophical methodology requires considering alternative explanations. After all, following Occam's razor, entities should not be multiplied beyond necessity.

There are three main alternatives to the mind hypothesis. The first is that the difference in personality is due to environmental factors.

While each clone is identical, they do not occupy the same space and hence have different experiences. These experiences result in differences in the brain and thus in the personalities. Countering this is the fact that many of the cloned animals are raised in the same conditions and such similarity in conditions should result in equally similar personalities.

Second, unlike in the movies, clones grow within the uterus of a 'mother' animal. Some scientists speculate that differences in personality can be accounted for by the fact that the animals grew in different uteruses and thus were exposed to different chemicals, experiences and other factors. Of course, this would not explain the difference between animals, such as the cloned pigs, which were in the same litter.

Third, there is the matter of epigenetics. As people are taught in high school biology, an animal has two copies of each gene – one from the mother and one from the father (these terms must be taken loosely in the case of clones). In some cases one gene or the other is disabled and this, presumably, could account for the differences. Countering this is the fact that epigenetics is still in its infancy, so its impact cannot be known at this time.

These alternatives do suggest an empirical test for the non-physical mind. If all these factors could be controlled adequately in a cloning experiment and the clones still had distinct personalities, then it would be even more reasonable to suspect that a non-physical mind exists.

Ghosts and minds

Everyone has heard of ghosts. Many people believe in them. However, there has not been a great deal of serious philosophical speculation on ghosts. This is not to say that there has been none, since the philosophical issue of ghosts was first discussed in Plato's *Phaedo*.[8] The purpose of this provocation is to consider the issue of the existence of ghosts within the context of modern philosophy of mind.

Before it can be decided whether ghosts can exist or not, one must be clear on what it is to be a ghost. For the purpose here, a ghost is a mind which has become disembodied through the death of its original body, yet still has the capacity to interact with the physical world in some manner. This interaction might be that the ghost can be sensed by others or that the ghost can actually manipulate its physical environment or perhaps there is some other capacity for interaction.

It should be noted that it has not been assumed that a ghost must be an immaterial entity. This is because assuming that ghosts must be immaterial would beg the question at hand. Thus, the possibility that ghosts could be material entities (of a special sort) must be kept open.

There are a variety of philosophic theories which attempt to explain the mind. Some of the more popular and famous ones include the identity theory, substance dualism, property dualism and functionalism. The implications of these theories will be considered in turn.

Identity theory is a materialist theory of mind, which is to say that it is a view that takes the mind to be composed of matter. More specifically, those who accept the identity theory assert that each mental state is identical to a state of the central nervous system. Thus, the mind is equivalent to the central nervous system and its states. Given the nature of identity theory, it is clear that if it is correct, then there are no ghosts. This is because the death of the central nervous system would be the death and end of the mind, because they are identical.

Substance dualism is the view that reality contains at least two fundamental types of entities: material entities and immaterial entities. On this view, which was most famously presented by Descartes,[9] the mind is an immaterial substance which enjoys a special sort of causal relation with its body. This rather mysterious relation enables the mind to control and receive information from the body and allows the body to affect the mind in some respects. Not surprisingly, on this view ghosts are a real possibility. Since the mind is taken to be a separate substance, the death of the body need not result in the death of the mind. Since the mind is a distinct substance and substances are entities that are capable of independent existence, the mind could, in theory, continue to exist. Further, since the mind is assumed to be able to interact with its original body, it is also possible that the mind could continue to interact with the physical world even in its bodiless state. Presumably, the lack of a physical body could limit what the mind was capable of, which might explain why ghosts are often taken to be limited in their capabilities. For example, it is typically believed that ghosts are often limited to making faint noises, moving small objects, or creating annoying thumping and banging noises.

A second type of dualism is sometimes referred to as property dualism. On this view, the mind and body are not distinct substances. Instead, the mind is composed (at least in part) of mental properties that are not identical with physical properties. For example, the property of *being a painful feeling* could not be reduced to a particular physical property of the brain, such as the states of certain neurons. Thus, the mind and body are distinct, but are not different substances.

Property dualism has a long history and, not surprisingly, there are many varieties of this view. It splits, roughly, into two main camps, epiphenomenalism and interactionism. One of these is consistent with the existence of ghosts, the other is not.

Epiphenomenalism is the view that there is a one-way relation between the mental and physical properties. On this view, the nonphysical mental properties are caused by, but do not in turn cause, the physical properties of the body. Thus, the mind is causally inert and is, crudely speaking, a by-product of the physical processes of the body. Because the mental properties are causally dependent on the physical properties, the death of the body will result in an end to the mental properties. Hence, if epiphenomenalism is correct, then there are no ghosts.

Interactionism is, in this context, the view that the mental properties of the mind and physical properties of the body interact. On this view, mental properties can bring about changes in the physical properties of the body and vice versa. Unlike epiphenomenalism, interactionism does not require that the mental properties be entirely causally dependent on the physical properties of the original body. Because of this, the mental properties that compose the mind could, in theory, survive the death of the original body. These mental properties might be capable of existing as a bundle of properties. In this case, a ghost would be a bundle of mental properties that form a mind without any physical body. The mental properties might require some substance or body to support them. In this case, a ghost would be a mind that consists of mental properties that are supported by something other than its original body. For example, the mental properties might inhere in an object or place. This might explain the fact that ghosts are typically said to haunt particular places. If their minds inhere in these places, this would explain why ghosts rarely, if ever, travel about the world. As another possibility, the mental properties might take control of a new body. This might explain cases that purportedly involve possession. In any case, since the mental properties are supposed to be capable of interaction with physical properties, it would be possible for the mind to continue to interact with the physical world, despite the death of its original body.

One last view to be considered is functionalism. There are many varieties of functionalism, but they all share a common basis. This basis is that mental states are defined in functional terms. Roughly put, a functional definition of a mental state defines that mental state in terms of its role or function in a mental system of inputs and outputs. To be a bit more specific, a mental state, such as being in pain, is defined in terms of the causal relations that it holds to external influences on the body, other mental states, and the behaviour of the body.

Functionalism is typically regarded as a materialist view of the mind. This is because the systems in which the mental states take place are taken to be physical systems. While the identity theory and functionalism are both materialist theories of mind, they differ in one key respect. According to the identity theorists, a specific mental state, such as being in pain, is identical to a specific physical state, such the state of neurons in a particular part of the brain. So, for two mental states to be the same, the physical states must be identical. Thus, if mental states are particular states of neurons in a certain part of the human nervous system, then anything that does not have that sort of nervous system cannot have a mind. According to the functionalist, a specific mental state, such as being in pain, is not defined in terms of a particular physical state. Instead, while the functionalist believes that every mental state is a physical state of some kind, for two mental states to be the same they need only be functionally identical, not physically identical. Thus, if mental states are defined functionally, then anything that can exhibit these functions can have a mind.

As odd as it might sound, if functionalism is the correct theory of mind, then it is still possible for ghosts to exist. This is the case even if it is assumed that functionalism must be a materialist theory of mind. As noted above, functionalism is committed to the view that any system that performs the proper functions is a mind, regardless of how that system is constituted. Given this, it seems possible that a mind could suffer the loss of its original physical system, yet still retain the same or adequately similar functions after this loss. Since the mind is, on the functionalist account, a physical system, there would be no special problem with it interacting with the physical world, even after it has a new physical system. The new physical system might be a structure, place or a new body. For example, a person might die in a house and, consistent with many ghost stories, the mind of the person might survive in the house. In functionalist terms, the mind that was once a set of functions instantiated in a human body would now be a set of functions instantiated in a house or parts of a house. As long as the functions are preserved, the mind would continue to exist as a ghost. Since ghosts are typically said to be confined to particular places, even particular rooms, the functionalist account of ghosts has a certain plausibility.

While the issue of the actual existence or non-existence of ghosts has not been settled, this discussion has addressed the issue of the existence of ghosts within the context of modern philosophy of mind. If dualism, interactionism or functionalism is correct, then ghosts can exist. However, if identity theory is correct, then there can be no ghosts.

Mind and medicine

One long-standing philosophic problem is the relation of mind and body. While there are many philosophic positions on this subject, they can be divided into two main camps. The first camp, dualism, is the view that mind and body are distinct entities of fundamentally different kinds: the mind is a non-material entity and the body is composed of matter. The second is monism, which is a denial of the dualist division. The most commonly accepted version is material-ism – the view that all that exists is matter. On this view there is no mind–body distinction because there are only bodies. This view does not deny the existence of brains – just the existence of non-material minds.

While medical science has generally focused on the treatment of the body, a fairly recent trend has been to investigate the relation between the mind and the body. Recent investigations into the effects of placebos appear to shed some light on the problem at hand and these findings will be discussed.

While people generally think of sugar pills when they think of placebos, one test of the placebo effect involved arthroscopic knee surgery.[10] Patients were divided into two groups: one received real surgery and the other received 'fake' surgery, but believed they had been treated. Oddly enough, the patients who underwent the 'fake' surgery enjoyed greater mobility than those who had received the actual surgery.

A second test involved Parkinson's patients.[11] Their condition involves a reduction of their motor functions due to the brain failing to produce a neurotransmitter. Amazingly enough, when the patients were told that they were being treated, their brains began to produce the neurotransmitter – despite the fact that the 'treatment' was merely an injection of saline solution.

A third test, conducted by psychologist Tor Wager,[12] involved telling subjects they would be tested with two types of cream: one would reduce pain and the other would not. The test subjects reported that the pain reducing cream worked as promised and this was confirmed by scans of their brains. Of course, the 'two' creams were the same.

A fourth test showed that the placebo effect can also produce negative results – this is sometimes called the 'nocebo' effect. Patients involved in a trial were given a placebo and informed they might experience gastrointestinal problems. As it turned out, these patients suffered more distress than those who took the placebo without being informed of its 'side-effects'.

A fifth test involved the use of virtual reality. One recent test involved burn patients using a program called SnowWorld[13] via a VR headset (basically a monitor one wears). Verbal reports and MRIs showed that the use of SnowWorld significantly reduced the brain activity associated with pain.

In light of these tests, a case could be made for the existence of the mind. First, there is the matter of the language used to describe these tests. Interestingly, the press and even medical professionals discuss the placebo effect in terms of the mind affecting the body. Given this fact, it seems somewhat reasonable to conclude that the mind does exist.

Second, there appears to be a difference in kind at work in such situations. Surgery and the use of real drugs have clear physical effects on the body. In sharp contrast, merely telling a patient she is receiving treatment does not seem to involve such clear physical cause and effect. Rather, something else seems to be involved and perhaps this is the mind.

In further support of the difference, consider what would happen if one told a poorly running car that is was being treated and then used a placebo on it. Obviously, the placebo would have no effect on the car. One plausible explanation for the distinction between humans and cars is that cars lack minds while humans have them. Hence placebos work on humans and not on cars.

Of course, replies can be made to these arguments. First, simply because medical professionals talk about the mind–body interaction it does not follow that the mind exists. After all, people talk about demons and ghosts, yet one would not then conclude they must exist. Further, the use of 'mind' could simply be shorthand for the brain and nervous system or merely sloppy use of language -- it need not be concluded that those using the term are committed to metaphysical dualism.

In regards to the second argument, an analogy can be drawn between a human being and a computer. A computer is a purely physical system, yet it would be possible to create a negative placebo effect in a computer. For example, a mouse that is really damaged will not work. But, the computer can be told via software that the mouse is not working, even though it is 'physically' fine. This is analogous to the situation in which a person believes she is ill when, in fact, she is not. A similar sort of programming trick could be done to create an analogue to a positive placebo effect. In this case, the computer (like a human patient) would regard the hardware as more damaged than it actually is and then be programmed to accept that this is not the case, thus utilizing the hardware that was previously detected as damaged. Thus, there is no need to postulate the existence of an immaterial mind – all that is needed is a programmable system (be it a brain or a CPU) and a body (be it hardware or organic).

Given these arguments, it seems reasonable to conclude that these cases do not conclusively show that the mind exists – after all, they can be explained without involving immaterial minds. They do show that there is clearly an interaction between the nervous system and the rest of the body, but whether this also involves an extra element remains to be seen.

Politics and belief

It is generally known that people tend to believe what they want to believe – even in the face of overwhelming evidence to the contrary. People even go so far as to downplay and ignore evidence against what they believe while modifying and even fabricating evidence to support their own view. Thinkers have often speculated on why this is the case and, thanks to researchers at Emory University,[14] the physiology behind this process was revealed at the 2006 conference for the Society for Personality and Social Psychology.

Just prior to the 2004 American Presidential election, the Emory researchers studied 15 devoted Republicans and 15 devoted Democrats. While a functional magnetic resonance imaging device was scanning their brains they were asked to assess claims made by Kerry and Bush. All the candidates contradicted themselves in these claims. Each group was critical of the opposing candidate while being very forgiving of their own.

The scans revealed that the part of the brain associated with reasoning was fairly inactive when members of a group examined the claims. Instead, the parts of the brain associated with emotion processing, conflict resolution and moral judgements were very active. Finally, when a subject rendered the judgement they found emotionally comfortable, the part of the brain associated with pleasure became active. Put roughly, the subjects did not rationally examine the claims. Instead, they went through a mental process that rewarded them for believing the conclusion they wanted to believe.

Interestingly, this research seems to reveal that the subjects possessed critical thinking skills but selectively applied them. Specifically, they recognized the contradictions but assessed them on emotional rather than critical grounds. The subjects were critical of the person they disagreed with and forgiving of the person they supported and assessed their claims accordingly. This behaviour violates one of the most basic rules of critical thinking, namely that claims are to be assessed on their own merit and not on the basis of how one feels about them or their source.

If this sort of behaviour were limited to the 30 test subjects, then the results would be interesting but hardly cause for concern. However, this sort of thing is quite widespread. One excellent example is the matter of Iraqi weapons of mass destruction. After $900 million and 16 months of investigation the best inference from the evidence is that there were no WMDs present when the United

States invaded Iraq in 2003. However, a Harris Poll published on 21 July 2006[15] revealed that 50 per cent of those polled believed that Iraq had WMDs when the US invaded. Interestingly only 36 per cent of those polled believed this in 2005 and only 38 per cent in 2004. Since no new evidence regarding the existence of WMDs has been forthcoming, this change in belief must be based on some other factors.

One obvious factor is outright deception and manipulation on the part of politicians and the news media. For example, despite the evidence, the Bush Administration is only willing to admit that 'perhaps' there were no WMDs in Iraq. As another example, on 21 July 2006, Fox News used the headline 'Are Saddam Hussein's WMDS Now in Hezbollah's Hands?'[16] While this unsupported headline was obviously too late to influence the poll, it does indicate the sort of manipulation that persists in the media.

Of course, the question arises as to why people allow themselves to be manipulated and why they elect to reject overwhelming evidence. One reason is partisanship. Not surprisingly, the majority of those who believe that Iraq had WMDs are Republicans. A second reason is that as the situation in Iraq grows steadily worse, Americans increasingly want to believe there was a good reason why America invaded. In short, people believe in Iraqi WMDs because doing so makes them feel better.

From a philosophical perspective, this situation is interesting because it reveals much about how and why people believe and reason (or fail to reason). It also makes it clearer what sort of challenge philosophers face in teaching people critical thinking skills and motivating them actually to make use of them. It also shows just how important it is for people to learn and apply these skills. While Iraq is but one example, it clearly shows the terrible price the world pays when people believe what they want to believe rather than what is supported by the evidence.

2   God and Purpose

Religion has apparently been around as long as humans, and debates over religion probably began shortly after the first religion appeared. In recent years much of the religious debate has centred on the conflict between the view that the universe was created and the denial of that view. In this sub-section God, religion and evolution are examined and used, as God intended, to provoke. Also included is an examination of the power of prayer.

Does God hate?

A number of people explicitly claim that God hates, although the alleged objects of his hatred tends to vary from person to person. Perhaps the most infamous group proclaiming God's hate is God Hates Fags.[17] These are probably best known for showing up at military funerals and claiming that God is killing American soldiers because he hates homosexuals and hence America. While this behaviour is reprehensible it does raise interesting philosophical and theological questions. The main question is: does God hate?

There are, of course, passages in the Bible that state that God hates and abominates various things ranging from shellfish (Leviticus 11:12) to homosexuality (Leviticus 18:22). If the Bible is an authoritative source on God, then it would seem that God does, in fact, hate. Of course, the Bible is riddled with factual errors and contradictory claims which makes it something less than a reliable source of information. It also seems fundamentally irrational to believe a textual source simply because some assert that it is the word of God. After all, if they know it is the word of God, then they certainly should be able to reveal how they know this to be true. If they can reveal how they know, then it would be possible for other people to verify this knowledge. In this case, the authority would not rest on the text – it would rest on the proof that the text is, in fact, true. Unfortunately, such proof seems to be sorely lacking. Fortunately, it is possible to bypass this thorny issue and address the question of God's hate with the use of reason.

God is alleged to be all-good, all-powerful and all-knowing. Assuming these traits, it would seem that God does not hate.

Intuitively, hatred seems to be incompatible with moral perfection. Those people who are regarded as being the best of humanity do not hate. Assuming that God should be at least as good as a human being, then it would seem to follow that he should not hate. Further, hatred seems to be a defect in character – a vice. If God is perfect in his goodness, then he has no vices. Of course, comparing God to humans can be somewhat problematic.

A second argument against God hating anything in the world is the fact that he is alleged to be all-powerful. This trait seems incompatible with hatred. For example, imagine you are outside talking to someone. She tells you that she hates mosquitoes and mosquito bites. Yet, each time a mosquito lands on her arm to bite her, she does nothing. You would suspect that she does not know what the word means, is somehow unable to move or is insane. If she truly hated mosquitoes and had the power to eliminate them, then there would be no mosquitoes biting her. By analogy, if God hates something, then he would see to it that what he hates did not exist. Being all-powerful, nothing can exist or happen that he does not will or at least permit. So, if God hated homosexuals, there would be no homosexuals. If God hated America, there would be no America.

At this point an obvious counter is the stock free-will reply – people can choose to do things that God hates because he gave us free will.

Of course, the free will is free to choose only among the various options that God has provided. After all, since he is supposed to be the all-powerful creator, he decides what options are ultimately available to humans. For example, if God had not made homosexuality an option, then people would not be able to choose it (assuming it is a choice, which seems unlikely).

Obviously, since God makes those options available, then he bears responsibility for making those options available and hence it would be a bit odd for him to hate and punish people for choosing one of his options. To use an analogy, suppose a parent who hates cake sets a cake and a bowl of broccoli in front of her child. She then tells the child that she can choose between the two. The child chooses the cake and then the parent hates and punishes the child. Intuitively, that seems to be unjust – if the child will be punished for eating cake, then cake should not be placed before the child. Likewise, if God truly hates homosexuality, then that should not be available as an option.

It can be replied that God must provide options that he hates in order for free will to truly be free. If God did not provide options that he hated, then human beings would not be free.

This reply does have some appeal – the greater the options, the greater the freedom. However, a problem still arises because God is supposed to hate and punish people who choose options that God hates. Unfortunately for humans, God does not provide clear and distinct warnings about what he hates. If God is perfectly good, then humans should have a mechanism that warns them without fail when they are about to take an action that God hates and for which God will punish them.

It might be countered that moral ignorance, like legal ignorance, is no excuse. But in this situation it would be a perfectly good excuse. Unlike human authorities, God is all-powerful, so he could make it so that we unfailingly know what he hates. This knowledge would not interfere with our free will in the least since we would still be free to select among the various options. The only difference would be that the choices would be informed choices.

It might be objected that God does let people know what he hates through scriptures and our own moral sense. However, not everyone has or has had access to the scriptures and the human moral sense is rather unreliable. It would be rather unfair of God to put in options he hates, provide us with a terribly unreliable mechanism for sorting out these options and then punish us for our violations. If he does this, then he is not all-good. It might be asserted that he cannot provide us with a reliable means of knowing what he hates. But if he cannot provide us with a reliable means of knowing what he hates, then he is not all-powerful.

There is an easy way out of this problem: accepting that God does not hate. The world is exactly as he wants it and we do not have a reliable means of determining what God hates because he does not hate anything. Not even America.

Evolution, analogy and complexity

Although in the past philosophers and scientists presented arguments to show that the universe resulted from intelligent design, this view seems to have almost completely fallen out of favour. In fact, in its July 2002 issue *Scientific America* roundly dismissed attempts to argue for intelligent design as 'nonsense'.

My purpose in this brief provocation is to address, from a philosophic standpoint, John Rennie's reply to the complexity argument in '15 Answers to Creationist Nonsense'.[18] Presented a bit more robustly than in the article, the argument is as follows: From the standpoint of probability, it is effectively impossible for any suitable complex entity to evolve by a process governed solely by chance. Since there are complex entities, it follows that there must be something other than chance governing the universe. This 'something other' must be an intelligent being.

Rennie replies that while chance factors into evolution, natural selection makes use of changes that are not random. It does this by ensuring the continuance of 'adaptive features' and discarding 'non-adaptive features'. He notes that 'as long as the forces of selection stay constant, natural selection can push evolution in one direction and produce sophisticated structures in surprisingly short times'.

From a philosophic standpoint, one of the most interesting parts of his reply is the analogy he employs. He notes that random chance (in the form of the famous million monkeys equipped with typewriters) would take up to 78,800 years to produce the famous phrase 'TOBEORNOTTOBE'. However, as he points out, Richard Hardison wrote software that could create phrases randomly but would also, most importantly, maintain the position of individual letters that 'happened to be correctly placed'. Unlike the poor million monkeys, the program produced the phrase in 336 attempts and in under a minute and a half. Given four and a half days, the program was able to reconstruct *Hamlet*.

At first glance, this analogy seems to be a powerful argument in defence of the claim that complex entities can be built up out of the combination of a random process and a non-random method of selection. And, at second glance, it can be seen that this is exactly what it is.

However, the analogy creates an interesting problem. One key claim in evolutionary theory is that there is, in fact, no intelligent design behind the process of selection and evolution – the process is not entirely random but it is not guided by or the product of an intelligent being (or beings). This is not to say, of course, that intelligent beings, like humans, do not intervene in the process through selective breeding and genetic engineering.

Now, what is interesting about the analogy is that while the program does illustrate a system in which complexity is generated via non-random selection, it is also obviously the product of intelligent design. If the program is taken as being analogous to the universe in which natural selection does its business, then Hardison must be taken as being analogous to the legendary intelligent designer who has laid down the mechanism of evolution and who has given it a purpose (in this case, to re-create the play). Thus, in a twist of irony, the analogy actually serves to support the claim that the universe is the product of intelligent design.

It might be contended that it is somehow unfair to focus on the fact that the software is the product of intelligent design and that what should be focused on is how the software illustrates a particular mechanism. In reply, the point at issue is whether or not complex entities require an intelligent designer to take a role in some part of the process that results in said entities. Hence, if it is claimed that intelligent design is not needed, than an analogy must be presented that does not involve intelligent design in the process. Naturally, evolution cannot be presented as an analogy to itself – this would beg the question. Perhaps paradoxically, no experiment can be set up by intelligent agents to prove that complex entities can arise without the benefit of intelligent design – by setting up the experiment they have already become the intelligent designers.

First God, then the mind

The existence of an intelligent designer has been long debated – presumably by intelligent beings. While many have argued against an intelligent designer, they probably did not realize that one of their arguments could be used to argue against the existence of intelligent beings. The idea is that if we do not need to postulate an intelligent designer to explain the universe, we do not need to postulate intelligent beings to explain human behaviour. Those familiar with politics probably already believe this.

One classic argument for the existence of an intelligent designer is the argument from design. The basic idea is that the existence of an intelligent designer can be inferred from the apparent design of the world.

One of the more sophisticated arguments in this family is based on the earth being ideally fine-tuned for life. Given the amazing complexity of the earth and the life upon it, untold numbers of factors would have to be, as Goldilocks would say, 'just right'. Given the incredible odds of this occurring by chance, it is reasonable to infer an intelligent designer.

The standard response to this is based on a consideration of the size of the universe and basic probability. Even if the odds that a specific planet will be 'just right' are incredibly slim, the odds of there being a planet that is 'just right' will increase as the number of planets increases. Given the incredible size of the universe and the evidence for planets orbiting other stars, it is reasonable to accept that life could have emerged by unguided chance. The next step is to apply Occam's razor[19] (one should not multiply entities beyond necessity) and accept the chance hypothesis over the existence of an intelligent designer.

A way to counter this is to change the focus from earth to something a bit larger – the entire universe. Like earth, the universe seems fine-tuned for our existence. For example, if the electromagnetic force were slightly weaker, hydrogen would not exist, so there would be neither normal stars nor water – and thus no humans. Given that the universe is 'just right' and the incredible odds of this occurring without guidance, it seems reasonable to accept an intelligent designer.

While it might seem a rather bold enterprise, this counter can be countered by postulating the existence of many universes. Even if the odds that a specific universe would be 'just right' are almost inconceivably small, the odds that there is a universe that is 'just right' will increase in proportion to the number of universes. Fortunately for the argument, many physicists and cosmologists claim that a multitude of universes exists.

While Occam's razor might seem to cut in favour of intelligent design over a multitude of universes, the razor is a metaphysical injunction against multiplying the kinds of entities. Having multiple universes still involves only one kind of entity. Having one universe and an intelligent designer involves two kinds of entities. Hence, the multiple universe hypothesis has the advantage over the intelligent design hypothesis.

Given that the above argument has successfully rid the universe(s) of the intelligent designer, it seems reasonable to take the argument to its logical conclusion and rid the universe(s) of all intelligence.

While there is significant disagreement over the nature and basis of intelligence, it is generally accepted that humans are intelligent beings. This is supported by the following reasoning. Some behaviour exhibited by human beings, such as speaking and constructing machines, seems to indicate the presence of intelligence. This is because it would be unreasonable to attribute such behaviour to unguided chance. For example, after reading this column one would infer it was written by an intelligent being rather than randomly generated by a program (or so I hope) because of the incredibly slim odds that something so complex could result from unguided chance.

This reasoning matches the argument from design – the existence of intelligence is inferred from what appears to be the product of intelligence. Thus, it is not surprising that this argument can be countered in the same way.

Even if the odds that creatures on a specific planet will behave (by unguided chance) in ways that seem intelligent are incredibly slim, the odds of there being such a planet will increase as the number of planets increases. Given the incredible size of the universe and the evidence for planets orbiting other stars, it seems reasonable to accept, given Occam's razor, that all apparently intelligent behaviour on earth is the result of unguided chance.

It might be believed that the existence of intelligence could be supported by finding other apparently intelligent beings. However, even if the entire universe were teeming with seemingly intelligent life, it should not be inferred that there are intelligent beings. As above, one needs but postulate the existence of many universes to counter that hypothesis. Even if the odds that a specific universe is inhabited by creatures that appear to behave intelligently are almost inconceivably small, the odds that there is a universe containing such creatures will increase in proportion to the number of universes. Given Occam's razor and a choice between a multitude of universes or accepting one universe containing intelligent beings, the multitude of universes is the one that must, rather ironically, be chosen.

Intelligent design and science

The debate over whether life is the result of a purposeless or purposeful process has once again made headlines in the United States. While the media tends to present the debate as a battle between scientists and creationists, the actual debate is more complex and involves numerous interesting and philosophical issues.

One interesting issue is whether or not an intelligent design theory can be considered a scientific theory. Naturally, the answer depends on the definition of 'science' and the specific intelligent design theory under consideration.

The version of intelligent design most often presented by popular media is a creationist account dressed up in scientific language. More sophisticated accounts of intelligent design date back to the earliest days of philosophy and include those of Plato and Aristotle. Despite their differences, such theories have a common element that serves to group them: such theories deny the claim that life is the result of a purposeless process that has no direction or goal. Naturally, the theories vary in their details. For example, Aristotle posits the existence of a First Mover[20] which is very different from the God presented in creationist accounts.

While these theories can be considered philosophical, whether they are scientific theories or not depends on the standards for classifying theories.

It is often assumed that a scientific theory must explain reality through purely natural causes. Some even claim that a scientific theory cannot include any entities that are non-physical. From a general philosophical standpoint, gravity would be a physical phenomenon. Examples of non-physical entities would include Platonic forms, Cartesian minds, and the traditional God.

The view that science deals solely with natural explanations and physical entities seems rather reasonable and enjoys a long tradition. This view was argued for by Descartes,[21] who famously divided reality into the physical (the domain of mechanistic science) and the mental (the domain of theology and religion). It does seem reasonable to divide fields by their subject matter: as French is distinct from geometry and chemistry, science should be distinct from theology and philosophy.

If the division is merely one of subject matter, in that science deals with purposeless phenomena and other disciplines handle purposeful phenomena, then there would be no debate over the status of intelligent design theories. They would all be, by definition, unscientific. This would be no more problematic than saying that the theory of gravity is not a literary theory.

However, the division is not merely one of subject matter. When a theory is classified as unscientific, this is a criticism that the theory is defective. After all, various 'crackpot' theories are rejected for being 'unscientific' even though they offer explanations in terms of purposeless physical processes. In such cases the flaws involve their failure to meet specific conditions that are taken as the hallmark of science, such as testability and explanatory power. These standards are well established and numerous arguments have been and can be given in their support. Thus, they are reasonable grounds for distinguishing between scientific and unscientific theories.

If being unscientific is seen as a defect, then it is unreasonable to use subject matter as the primary basis for distinguishing science from non-science. After all, this would involve question begging – simply being outside the subject area of science would make a theory defective. Instead, it seems reasonable to rely on non-question-begging standards like testability and explanatory power. If an intelligent design theory can meet those standards, it would be scientific.

Ironically, the scientific status of the 'standard' theory of evolution can be used to prove the scientific status of an intelligent design theory. The theory of evolution involves the claim that life is not the result of purposeful design and that evolution does not aim at a goal or end. An intelligent design theory accepts the opposite view.

One hallmark of a scientific theory is that its claims are testable: they can be confirmed or disconfirmed. Since the key claim of each theory is the denial of the other it follows that confirming one disconfirms the other. Thus, both claims fall within the realm of science – there is no principled way to claim that only the denial of purpose is a valid scientific hypothesis. Hence, it would seem that an intelligent design theory can be a scientific theory.

Threat by design?

In the 15 August 2005 issue of *Newsweek* Jonathan Alter[22] presents his criticism of and his concerns about intelligent design. While his essay is well reasoned it does contain some problems that, as a philosopher, I feel compelled to address.

One of Alter's main concerns is that the supporters of intelligent design are serving to undermine the future of science in America. He claims that one cause for the reduced number of American science majors is 'the pernicious right-wing notion that conventional biology is vaguely atheistic'.

While this concern is laudable and the dearth of science majors is cause for worry, it is unlikely that significant blame for this problem can be laid upon the proponents of intelligent design. As a professor I have numerous opportunities to speak with students about their choices in regards to majors. Based on this admittedly anecdotal evidence, the reason there are relatively few American science majors seems to have little, if anything, to do with fear of the taint of atheism. Instead, the main cause seems to be the fact that the sciences are often perceived as boring, difficult and not as lucrative as other fields (such as business). Further, even if some students did perceive biology as 'vaguely atheistic' this would hardly explain the dearth of majors in the other sciences.

More importantly, even if it is true that intelligent design is somehow linked to this decline, it does not follow that there is not an intelligent designer. This is because it is a fallacy to make inferences about the truth or falsity of a claim based on its consequences. We must be careful to distinguish between a concept and the uses to which some attempt to put it.

This is not to say that we should not be concerned about such consequences. If intelligent design is, in fact, such a serious threat, then perhaps it should be fought and rejected on pragmatic grounds. Naturally, there would be a certain irony in protecting science and reason on this basis.

Alter next turns to the stock argument from authority against intelligent design and cites President Bush's scientific advisor John H. Marburger III's assertion that 'Intelligent design is not a scientific concept.'[23] The idea is that since a scientific authority claims that intelligent design is not science, then it follows that it is not.

On the face of it, this is a reasonable argument – surely such an eminent scientist knows what is scientific and what is not. However, there are reasons to be concerned with this argument. First, there is the general concern that arguments from authority are inherently weak. Second, there are good arguments that intelligent design does fall in the realm of science. For example, one such argument was presented in the previous provocation. Hence, this appeal to authority is hardly conclusive.

As Alter points out, while most scientists reject intelligent design, it is not without its supporters. Perhaps its best-known defender is the Discovery Institute.[24] One of its members, Stephen Meyer, argues that intelligent design is based on an inference to the best explanation which he takes to be a basic scientific method.

In response, Alter takes the stock approach of acknowledging the intellectual merits of this view while at the same time banishing it to the realm of humanities – so as to protect true science. To be specific, he accepts that while this sort of thing is acceptable in a graduate class in philosophy of science, to use it to justify teaching intelligent design in ninth-grade biology classes is 'a cruel joke'.[25]

Alter does make a reasonable point – ninth-grade biology is probably not an ideal place to discuss the nuances of philosophy of science. Further, he does raise the legitimate concern that the attempts to include intelligent design in the classroom are most likely actually aimed at installing specific religious doctrines into the curriculum.

However, there is certainly something to be said about introducing students to the philosophy of science as part of their education – even in ninth grade. Further, an adequate understanding of the theory of natural selection would seem to require at least some vague familiarity with the worldview that it replaced and its main competition, namely that of a teleological universe.

Alter then presents the stock argument that the claim that complexity cannot be adequately explained by natural selection is 'unproven and probably unprovable'. He further asserts that intelligent design's performance in the laboratory is 'worse than medieval alchemy'.

This criticism has a reasonable basis: a hypothesis that cannot be tested (proven or disproven) cannot be considered a scientific hypothesis. However, Alter's criticism can be countered.

First, intelligent design does seem to be a testable hypothesis. Keeping things simple, if intelligent design is taken as the denial of natural selection in favour of purposeful selection, then it can be tested indirectly by testing natural selection. To the degree that there is evidence for natural selection, there would be evidence against intelligent design. This is, of course, based on Occam's razor – if evolution can be explained without a designer, there is no need to claim there is such a being. Assuming, as most scientists do, that natural selection has been shown to be all but certain, then it would follow that intelligent design (in this context) is a scientific, albeit seemingly disproven, hypothesis.

Second, it seems unreasonable to claim that the hypothesis of intelligent design is unprovable. Most scientists regard natural selection as a proven fact. If this is true, then scientists must be able to tell the difference between evidence for natural selection and evidence for design. If they cannot make this distinction, then the hypothesis of natural selection would, of course, be undercut because the relevant evidence would be in doubt. Assuming that scientists can recognize evidence for natural selection, then they would presumably also be able to recognize evidence for design. If this is the case, then the intelligent design hypothesis would be provable in the sense that supporting evidence would be recognizable. Of course, being provable merely means that it could be proven – it does not mean that it is or even will be proven.

Powerless prayer

Over the past decade the power of intercessory prayer was put to the test in the Study of the Therapeutic Effects of Intercessory Prayer (STEP).[26] The study was conducted with scientific rigour to determine the possible medical effects of distant prayer. STEP involved 1,802 cardiac bypass surgery patients who were divided into three groups. The members of the first and second groups participated in a double-blind study. The members of the first group were prayed for while those in the second were not. To avoid bias, neither the patients nor their doctors knew which group was being prayed for. The members of the third group were prayed for and were informed of this fact. The prayers were provided by two Catholic groups and by one Protestant group.

After the study was completed, analysis of the data revealed no significant difference between the two groups involved in the double-blind study. Interestingly, the third group fared the worst of the three – those who knew they were being prayed for suffered more complications than the members of the first two groups. Those conducting the study believe that the results in the third group can be explained by stress and anxiety: those who were informed they were the subject of prayers most likely believed that their condition was so dire that they needed prayer.

Given these results, the logical conclusion is that intercessory prayer is not causally efficacious. Informing someone they are being prayed for is apparently efficacious – but in a negative way. Given these results it is somewhat ironic that the majority of funds for STEP came from the John Templeton Foundation – an organization devoted to promoting religious beliefs.

A similar study, MANTRA II,[27] yielded the same results. This study, which also involved hundreds of cardiac patients, showed that intercessory prayer had no discernible medical effect.

While the studies are obviously scientifically and theologically interesting, they and the reaction they generated are also philosophically interesting.

From a scientific standpoint, the studies are fairly conclusive and it would seem to be irrational to continue to believe in the efficacy of intercessory prayer. However, the studies seem to have done little to change the minds of those who believe. Their view of the results seems to be best stated by a member of one of the prayer groups, Bart Barth. His response was that 'people of faith don't need a prayer study to know that prayer works'.[28]

This does raise an interesting philosophical problem about belief. From a rational standpoint, one should believe claims on the basis of reason and evidence. Given the care in which the studies were conducted, there is not much room for rational doubt in regards to the inefficacy of prayer in this context. Hence, it seems evident that reason is not what people of faith need to know that prayer works.

It must be noted that there is, of course, always some room for philosophical doubts. The apparent failure of prayer could be explained in a variety of ways that are consistent with the efficacy of prayer. A few examples are as follows. First, it could be that God only accepts prayers from certain people and the right people did not pray in the study. Second, it could be that he only accepts prayers presented in a certain manner and those praying in this study did not do it right. Third, it could be that he only responds to prayers said for the right sort of people.

While these are possible explanations, they are all also things that could be tested. Using the three examples, another study could be conducted with the right people saying the right sort of prayers for the right people. If the new study fails to show the efficacy of prayer, then another study could be conducted to take into account the explanations as to why the previous study failed to establish the power of prayer.

Naturally, this process could continue a very long time – there is almost always a way to come up with some possible reason why a study did not prove the efficacy of prayer. However, if prayer has any efficacy at all, then there would presumably be some way to discern this fact. If it is claimed that prayer is efficacious in ways that cannot be tested or discerned, it is quite reasonable to consider two problems. First, there would seem to be no way for anyone to know it was effective. Second, there does not seem to be any difference between something that has no effect at all and something whose alleged effect is in principle indiscernible and untestable. In such a scenario someone could still believe in the power of prayer, but it would seem that they would effectively have a belief without any content.

In light of the above, it might be wondered whether these studies serve to cast doubt on the existence of God. While it might be a matter of faith for some that God answers prayers, one bit of irony is that given the 'standard' philosophical conception of God it follows that intercessory prayer should not work. This point will be argued by comparing God to a human doctor.

One possible reason to think that intercessory prayer is effective is that it is needed to inform God. Just as a human doctor needs to be informed when she has patients in need, God needs to be informed when his aid is needed.

Unfortunately for this approach, God is generally taken to be omniscient. Given this assumption, prayer is not needed to inform God that someone is in need of his aid. He is, unlike a human doctor, always aware of everything. So, intercessory prayer cannot serve to inform God of something he is ignorant about. After all, God is not ignorant of anything.

Another possible reason to think that intercessory prayer is effective is that it is needed to persuade God to take action. While human doctors are supposed to be obligated to help, they are generally much more inclined to help those who can persuade them (typically via money) to take action. For example, the doctors who do cosmetic surgery for the rich are doing that instead of helping poor people with serious medical problems. The rich are not in greater need than the poor, they just have the means to motivate the doctors. In the case of God, he needs to be asked and persuaded by prayer to take action. On this view, God would presumably be motivated by factors such as the number, intensity and quality of the prayers and perhaps by other factors as well – such as the piety or the position in a church hierarchy of those praying.

Unfortunately for this view, God is generally taken to be morally perfect. Because of this, he would presumably not need to be persuaded or asked to do what is right – he would do what was right because it was right. Someone who has to be motivated by outside persuasion to do the right thing would hardly be morally perfect. Also, if God had to be motivated by prayers, then his actions in this regard would be contingent on factors that seem morally irrelevant – like whether the person's situation was known, whether he was known by enough and the right sort of people, and so forth. For example, a hermit who was injured far out in the woods would be out of luck, while a famous actress whose upcoming surgery was broadcast on the news would be in good shape prayer-wise. This would make God rather arbitrary and this seems inconsistent with his perfect goodness.

A third possible reason to think that intercessory prayer is effective is that it is needed to inform God that things are not going as we would like them so he can fix them.

In the case of human doctors, they can make mistakes or things can go wrong so that they need to be informed of these problems in order to correct them. However, this does not seem to apply to God. First, God knows everything so he presumably knows what we want or when things go wrong. Second, God is supposed to all-powerful. Everything that comes to pass is in accord with his will. So, if we are not getting what we want, then that is the way God wants it to be. If God did decide to change things, then we would have power over God – he would no longer be omnipotent.

In light of this argument, it is no surprise that intercessory prayer does not work. If God does not exist, it would obviously not work. If God exists and is as the philosophers and theologians claim, then it should not work. While there are other possibilities worth exploring, intercessory prayer does seem to be without power.

3 Scepticism

The arch-enemy of the traditional epistemologist is the sceptic – a person who denies that we have knowledge. There are excellent reasons to think that the sceptic cannot be defeated. Fortunately, scepticism is actually quite useful and hence there is nothing to worry about.

The unbreakable sceptic

Scepticism, in general, is the philosophic position that we do not have knowledge. There are various types of scepticism that are defined primarily by the extent of the doubt. For example, a very modest sceptic might doubt we can know whether metaphysical claims are true or not; while the most extreme sceptic would doubt everything – even her own existence. It is surprisingly easy to argue for scepticism and there are two arguments that seem effective against all attempts to argue that we do have knowledge.

The first argument is as follows. It is generally accepted that for a belief to count as knowledge it must be both true and adequately justified. Regardless of what standard of justification is used there will arise the question of what justifies the acceptance of that standard. If an attempt is made to justify that standard, then the question merely arises again for that attempt at justification. If no attempt is made to justify the standard, then there is no reason to accept the standard. Either way, there will be no grounds for accepting the standard and it will have to be concluded that the sceptic is right.

The enemy of the sceptic can counter by asserting that the standard is self-justifying or not in need of justification. Of course, this creates a bit of a problem: different people claim different self-justifying standards and use these to justify beliefs. Not surprisingly, these beliefs sometimes contradict one another. So, unless we are willing to accept contradictions, at least one of these standards must be flawed. To pick between them, we would need some sort of standard, which takes us back into the original problem. Not surprisingly, these standards sometimes contradict one another. So, to pick between them, we would need another standard, which takes us back to the original problem. This would, of course, place us in a pickle that might be worse than scepticism.

The second argument is as follows: for every reasonable argument given in support of the view that we have knowledge via some means there is a reasonable counter-argument that casts unbreakable doubt on that means. Ironically, these sceptical arguments can be based on the same sort of evidence used in the original argument. As an example, consider the senses. Suppose it is argued that we do know things via our senses because they are to be trusted – except under conditions in which we have reason to doubt them (such as when one has knocked back a few too many pints of beer). The sceptic can easily counter by the following argument: given that our senses are not infallible, how can it be determined when they are working properly and when they are not? Obviously, we cannot rely on our senses to answer this question – for they are what are in doubt. So, we need some new source of knowledge so that we can know our senses are to be trusted. But, of course, this alleged new source of knowledge can be countered as well.

The enemy of the sceptic could claim the existence of an infallible source of knowledge that is invulnerable to the gnawing teeth of sceptical doubt. Of course, not even this can stop the sceptic – there still arises the question of the means by which it can be determined that this source is infallible. If it is claimed that its infallibility is self-evident, a problem similar to the one raised above for self-justifying standards occurs – how do we choose among the various allegedly self-evident infallible sources of knowledge?

While there seems to be no effective way to beat the arguments for extreme scepticism, it is common for thinkers simply to reject such scepticism on pragmatic or evolutionary grounds, or to assert that we do know things. However, these attempts do not seem to succeed.

Clearly, simply asserting that we do know things begs the question for it assumes the sceptic is wrong without actually addressing the arguments. Of course, it has been contended by philosophers like Chisholm that it is perfectly acceptable to assume we know things and thus 'break' the sceptic.

Asserting that evolution, via natural selection, has produced beings that do have knowledge has a certain appeal. After all, an appeal to evolution seems to be an accepted (perhaps even orthodox) solution to a broad range of problems these days. However, this appeal merely pushes back the problem – in virtue of what is our belief in evolution justified? If we appeal to evolution again, we will have run in a circle. If we appeal to something else, then the initial appeal to evolution has been rejected. Either way, an appeal to evolution is no answer.

The pragmatic answer also has a certain appeal – assuming we know things seems to have practical value. Of course, the question still arises – in virtue of what is the belief in pragmatism justified? Obviously, it cannot be justified on pragmatic grounds and, if we appeal to something else, then the appeal to pragmatism has been abandoned.

Thus it would seem that the only way to 'break' the sceptical arguments is simply to assume they are ineffective. But there does not seem to be very much sport in that.

The value of extreme scepticism

Scepticism has a long and respectable tradition in philosophy, dating back (at the very least) to Socrates' claim that the only thing he knew was that he knew nothing. After Socrates,[29] Descartes[30] is probably the most famous sceptic. He claimed to be able to doubt everything except his own existence. Such runaway doubt can be dubbed 'extreme scepticism'. While Socrates and Descartes are still regarded with respect by most members of the philosophic community, extreme scepticism has fallen onto hard times. Most thinkers, often on the pragmatic grounds that it is useless, have rejected such scepticism. Yet such extreme scepticism is both defensible and useful.

It is relatively easy to raise sceptical doubts – even in regard to things that most people assume are beyond doubt. To follow the trail blazed by Descartes, it is a rather easy matter to raise doubts about our senses, about other minds and about there being an external world at all.

Normally, we trust our senses – so much so that people say, 'seeing is believing'. However, we have all experienced optical illusions and other phenomena that have taught us that our senses can deceive us. Given this fact, how can we know that we can trust them right now? We might assume that while our senses sometimes fail us, they work most of the time. Thus, you can be reasonably confident that you are reading this text, that another person wrote it and that there is a book in front of you. Or can you? You know you have thoughts and feelings, but you can only see other people's *behaviour*. Unlike Bill Clinton, you cannot *feel their pain*. So, how do you know that other people really have thoughts and feelings and are not just unfeeling, unthinking biological machines? The answer is, of course, you do not. If this situation isn't bad enough, consider this – you cannot even be sure that there is an external world. It is common for people (assuming they exist) to have dreams that seem quite real – until they wake up. How do you know that this is not one of those dreams? Obviously, you do not. For those who like science fiction, the dream scenario can be replaced with a computer-generated reality – as per *The Matrix* or the *Thirteenth Floor*. For those with a more philosophical bent, Descartes' evil demon can be used in place of the nefarious machines of *The Matrix*. In any case, there is no way to confirm that there is an external world of three-dimensional objects. Thus, it is a rather simple thing to cast doubt on our 'commonsense' view that our senses work reliably in a three-dimensional world that is inhabited by other people. Of course, the main question remains – scepticism is clever, but what use is it? It is to this matter that we now turn.

A significant number of people have no doubt at all about their beliefs – they accept and act on them without question. While most of these actions are harmless or even beneficial, some result in great harm. For example, some people accept and act upon racist beliefs – and these sometimes lead to systems of oppression or even attempts at genocide. Other people act upon political and religious beliefs that they do not question and sometimes this leads to terrible suffering and death. Much less extreme, but still of concern, is the fact that many people are trapped in dogmatic slumbers in which they simply accept beliefs based on their upbringing, tradition, peer pressure, habit, stereotypes, the media, and similar things. Conditioned to believe in things uncritically, such people are often easily swayed and manipulated. Sometimes they are transformed into dangerous true believers.

A reasonable cure for such unquestioning belief is, of course, doubt. Rational people who have doubts about their political or religious beliefs tend to be less inclined to do extreme or terrible things based on such beliefs. After all, they realize they could be wrong and this realization tends to put a degree of moderation in their actions. Naturally, this is not an infallible method. Sometimes when people feel doubt they redouble their efforts and steel their fanaticism in response. However, like medicine, doubt generally has more of a curative than harmful effect on people.

It is in the raising of doubt that scepticism excels. If a person realizes that even things that seem to be obviously and non-controversially true, like there being an external world, can be called into doubt, then they will be much less likely simply to take their other beliefs at face value. The practical problem is, of course, creating such doubt in people. Not surprisingly, the study of philosophy can help in this matter.

4 Love

Plato presented the first known philosophical discussion of love and people have been writing about it ever since. Not wishing to be outdone by Plato and Dr Phil (Phillip Calvin 'Phil' McGraw, psychologist and host of the hugely successful American TV show *Dr Phil*), I've contributed two pieces on this subject.

Who do you love?

While love has been addressed by thinkers ranging from Plato[31] to Dr Phil, the matter of the metaphysics and epistemology of love have not been given a great deal of attention. This brief provocation is presented in the hopes of rectifying this situation.

When one person, Jane, loves another, Dick, the question arises as to what it is exactly that she loves. The easy and obvious answer is that she loves Dick. But that simply raises questions about who Dick is and what it is about him that she loves.

In the ideal of romantic love, Jane would love Dick himself and not his qualities or possessions. After all, those qualities and possessions change and can also be possessed by others. Intuitively, we do not regard the ideal romantic love as something that will fade with change or something that can be transferred to another person with similar qualities. Such interchangeable love is obviously hardly romantic. What is needed, it would seem, is something that lies beneath all the qualities and possessions. This something would be what makes the person, in this case Dick, the person he is and separates him from all others.

Fortunately, such an entity is readily available in philosophy – it is known as a bare particular. A bare particular is a rather mysterious metaphysical entity. It is bare because it does not have any qualities of its own beneath all the qualities that it supports. It is a particular because there is only one of each (and each one can only be in one location at a time). In philosophical tradition the bare particular is supposed to be what distinguishes each individual thing for all other things. Such an entity would do quite nicely for the problem at hand. In ideal love one person simply loves the bare particularity of another as opposed to qualities or possessions that can change or be duplicated by another.

Unfortunately, there is a rather serious problem with this notion of love. When we interact with the world we interact with various qualities and properties. For example, Jane can see Dick in his bathing suit and she can see his bank account balance. But it would seem to be impossible for her to somehow be aware of his bare particularity. Since it has no qualities, there would seem to be nothing to experience. Given this, it simply does not seem possible for Jane to be aware of Dick's bare particularity in order to be in love with him. This would seem to take love back to being about detectable qualities.

Of course, having love rest on detectable qualities might not be so bad after all. In fact, it seems more realistic and intuitive than the idea of some sort of ideal metaphysically based concept of love. When one person talks about why she loves another, she will talk about the qualities the person possesses. Dating services also make a big deal about testing people for various qualities and using them to find compatibility and love. Many scientists talk about the emotion of love as being driven by genes in search of suitable genes to combine with – presumably this drive is aimed at particular empirical qualities. Given this evidence, it seems reasonable to conclude that when Jane loves Dick, she loves his qualities.

But even that does not seem quite right. One thing that philosophers and scientists have rather solidly established is that we do not perceive the world directly. While this description oversimplifies things greatly, we supposedly have neurological responses to physical objects that initiate sensory experiences in the mind or brain that are about such experiences. Put crudely, we do not experience things – we have ideas in our mind about things. If this view of perception is correct, then Jane does not love Dick directly. This is because she has never directly experienced Dick – all she has are her various perceptions that she takes to be of Dick.

A person's perceptions are, of course, interpreted by the person. To use an analogy, think of reading this text. What you initially experience are colours and shapes. These are then interpreted so that the colours and shapes become meaningful words. But what the words mean and how you react to them depends a great deal on you. You might find this provocation enlightening while another finds it annoying. Presumably the same thing happens with perceptions of people. So, when Jane says she loves Dick, she is actually saying that she is in love with her ideas of Dick. These ideas might or might not correspond to the real Dick. And, of course, in light of various sceptical worries about the existence of other minds or even the external world, there might not be any Dick at all. But, in the interests of sanity, such scepticism will be set aside.

While the notion that people actually love their ideas of other people might seem odd, it is plausible and does explain a great deal about relationships. Because of limits of space, only a couple of examples of how it explains things will be given. First, think of a situation in which Jane loves Dick but when she tells her friends why she loves him, her friends do not see Dick as having all (or even any) of those qualities. Assuming Jane is not insane, a reasonable explanation is that Jane's idea of Dick includes those qualities the actual Dick lacks. Second, think of situations in which Jane initially loves Dick and then says that Dick's sudden change put an end to her love. Yet, no one else notices that change in Dick. Assuming that Jane is not insane and that Dick is not cleverly concealing his change from everyone else, a reasonable explanation is that Jane's ideas about Dick changed and she has fallen out of love with her ideas and not Dick. Of course, she never loved Dick to begin with – only her idea of Dick.

So, on Valentine's Day rest assured that while you are not loved, there is a chance that someone does love the ideas they have of you.

Transcendent argument for true love

True love faces many obstacles. In the mythic past, these obstacles came between the lovers and took classic forms: fire-breathing dragons, feuding relatives, vile villains, high gas prices, or jealous rivals. Today, it is true love itself that is facing dire obstacles in the form of cynicism, science and philosophy.

While cynicism is a problem, science and philosophy pose the main intellectual challenges to true love. The challenge posed by science and philosophy is that good arguments in both fields point towards a denial of true love. Of course, one must determine what exactly is being denied.

While people vary greatly in their views of true love, the most basic element seems to be that true love is such that one person (Jane) loves another (Dick) himself and not his qualities or possessions. After all, qualities and possessions change and can be possessed by others. Intuitively, we do not regard true love as something that will fade with change or something that can be transferred to another person who happens to have similar qualities. For example, if Jane loves Dick because of his money or how he looks in a swimsuit, then she would presumably love Tom or Harry if they had the same (or more) money and looked equally good (or better) in a swimsuit. Such inter-changeable love is obviously not true love. What is needed is some-thing that lies beneath all the qualities and possessions. This would be what makes the person the person he is and separates him from all others. Unfortunately, it is just this sort of thing that contempor-ary scientists and philosophers tend to deny.

According to the received scientific view, love is a brain state that is ultimately driven by genes in search of suitable genes with which to combine. Naturally, this drive is aimed at particular empirical qualities and not some mysterious metaphysical entity. Put roughly, romantic love is just an evolutionary result that has been selected because it has enabled propagation of the species. So, if Dick loves Jane, this means that the organism that is Dick is reacting to the organism that is Jane in a way that would incline Dick to mate with

Jane. Whether or not Jane reciprocates would depend on the way her brain states respond to Dick's qualities. True love, in the classic sense, is obviously absent.

From a philosophical standpoint, what would be needed for true love is an underlying metaphysical self – the true self. This self would be the object of true love. However, as was argued in the previous provocation, there are serious problems with this approach. In light of these arguments, true love would seem to be as much a fantasy as fire-breathing dragons and honest politicians.

Despite the ravages of science, philosophy and the tabloids, people still want to believe in true love. In fact, it could be argued that most human beings need to believe in the possibility of true love. For whatever reason, people generally want to believe that they love and are loved – and that love is more than just an evolutionary device for the propagation of the species.

While making the world safe for true love is a daunting task, the first step in the process has already been taken by Immanuel Kant.[32] This first step involves arguing for the foundation of true love – the true, metaphysical self.

Kant famously divided the world into noumena and phenomena. The phenomena are the things as they appear to us. This is what we experience – such as seeing how Jane looks in a bikini. We can have empirical, scientific knowledge of such things. The noumena are the things in themselves. Kant argued that the noumena cannot be known because they are beyond our experience. Hence, the noumena cannot be the subject of science – they are beyond its legitimate bounds.

Logically, it would seem that we should just stick with the phenomena and withhold any speculation about the noumena. However, Kant claims that we cannot help but try to extend our reason beyond the realm of phenomena and into the realm of noumena. Because of this we are drawn to accept transcendent illusions of metaphysics.

One transcendent illusion, and a crucial one for true love, is the metaphysical self. Like the Scottish philosopher David Hume, Kant agrees that we can have no impression of the metaphysical self. What we do have are impressions, via introspection, of the empirical self. Put another way, when a person looks inside their 'mind' they never encounter a metaphysical self. What they encounter are various sensations, thoughts and feelings.

However, Kant argues that we have to think of our experiences as if they occur within a unified self. Doing this provides us with a frame of reference for thought and he argues that it is useful to accept a metaphysical self. Since it is useful and we need the metaphysical self to make sense of things, Kant concludes that we should accept the metaphysical self. There is, however, some debate over whether he thought we should treat it is a useful fiction or actually accept its existence based on his transcendent argument.

Returning to love, his argument can obviously be employed to argue for the self of true love. This is the self that is loved for what it truly is and loves others for what they truly are. This would, of course, be the metaphysical self.

It is also possible to use true love to support the existence of the metaphysical self using an argument modelled on Kant's case for God, freedom and immortality. In his argument, Kant contends that these three cannot be proven and hence cannot be known. But he claims that they are irresistible because they are necessary conditions for morality. Hence we must accept them.

Applying this method to true love, the argument would be as follows: as has been argued, true love would be impossible without the metaphysical self. As such, it is a necessary condition for true love. The metaphysical self is obviously beyond the realm of scientific proof. However, true love is irresistible because it seems to be a critical belief for our happiness and for our conception of ourselves as beings who are more than just rutting beasts. Thus, true love compels us to accept the existence of the metaphysical self.

Thanks to Kant, the world is now a safer place for true love. Now, if something could only be done about Dr Phil.

5   Time and Chance

The nature of time and whether the universe contains chance are two fundamental matters in metaphysics.

Meeting yourself

Travel, of any kind, involves journeying from one point to another point. In the case of spatial travel, this involves journeying from one location in space to another location. This sort of travelling happens all the time. For example, millions of people make the trip from the fridge to the sofa each day. Time travel, being a form of travel, also involves journeying from one point to another. However, in the case of time travel, the journey is made from one point in time to another point in time. While it might seem an odd sort of thing to say, time travel is happening all the time. In fact, you are doing it right now. Even as you read this sentence you are travelling towards the future at the rate of 60 minutes per hour. Of course, that sort of time travel is not what most people find interesting. One of the more interesting types of time travel involves moving from the present time to the past. Another interesting type of time travel is going into some future time, without all that time-consuming mucking about between now and then.

While it has been claimed that if a person travels far enough, she will end up back where she started, no one claims that if you travel far enough you will meet yourself. However, if time travel is possible, a person should be able to travel back in time and, in theory, meet herself in the past. If a person takes care not to travel too far ahead in time, he should be able to meet himself in the future.

Naturally, there are all sorts of problems and paradoxes involved with people travelling about in time to meet themselves. For example, suppose Bill, who is 34 now, decides to go back in time and kill himself at age 20. Obviously, if Bill succeeds in killing himself, he would not exist at age 34. Hence, he could hardly go back to kill himself. Yet, if Bill is able to travel through time, he should be able to go back and kill himself. These sorts of problems probably help fuel the sale of aspirin.

Fortunately, this section is not about those brain-teasing paradoxes. For example, I will not argue whether Bill would be committing murder or suicide if he went back in time to kill himself. Instead, I will focus on the problem of simply going back in time and meeting yourself. Or your past self. Or however one would word it.

As has been noted above, if you can travel backwards in time, then you should be able to meet yourself. This creates an interesting metaphysical problem: that of explaining how the very same thing, namely you, can be in two places at exactly the same time.

In order for the same person to be in two different places at the same time, the components that make up the person would, of course, have to be capable of existing in more than one place at the same time. In other words, the components would have to be capable of multiple location.

Another philosophic problem, namely the problem of universals, also involves the issue of the same thing existing in different places at the same time. Very, very briefly, one part of the problem of universals is determining what it is for two tokens to be of the same type. To give a concrete example, part of the problem would be determining what it is for six different green objects to all be the same in respect to their colour. Two popular solutions to the problem of universals, as it relates to the possibility of entities existing in multiple locations at the same time, are as follows.

David Armstrong, a well-known Australian philosopher, argues that there are instantiated universals.[33] Briefly, an instantiated universal is a property (such as *being green*) that can exist in multiple locations at the same time. Going back to the problem of universals, for six different objects to all be green would be for each object to instantiate the universal green. The very same, identical universal green would be wholly located at each green object. To be even more specific, if a frog and a leaf are the same shade of green, the green of the frog and the green of the leaf are one and the same entity which happens to be multiply located.

Now, suppose that whatever it is that makes a person the person he happens to be is composed of instantiated universals. (If, for example, a person is her soul, the soul would be composed of universals.) In this case it would seem that going back in time to meet yourself would be possible. What would make this possible? First, it has been assumed that what makes a person who he is, say Bill, is made up of universals. Second, a universal, as has been established, is capable of existing in distinct locations at the same time. Hence, the universals that make up the person Bill happens to be can exist in different places at the same time. So, it would be possible to have a person identical to Bill standing five feet from Bill. This identical person could be the Bill from the future. Since Bill and Bill from the future would be identical, then it would seem they would be the same person. Hence, if a person is composed of universals, then he could travel back in time to meet himself. It would simply be a case of the same person existing in different locations at the same time.

Keith Campbell[34] and I, among others, reject instantiated universals in favour of tropes. Briefly, a trope is a property (such as *being green*) that can only exist in one location at one time. Trope theorists explain what it is for two tokens to be of the same type in terms of resemblance. As an example, for six different objects to all be green would be for each object to have its own distinct green trope. Each green trope would be a different entity from the other green tropes, but they would resemble each other and would all be taken to be green because of their resemblance.

Now, suppose that what makes a person the person he happens to be is composed of tropes. In this case it would seem that going back in time to meet yourself would be impossible. What would make this impossible? First, it has been assumed that what makes a person who she is, say Sally, is made up of tropes. Second, a trope, as has been established, is incapable of existing in distinct locations at the same time. Hence, the tropes that make up Sally cannot exist in different places at the same time. So, it would not be possible to have a person identical to Sally, say the Sally from the future, standing five feet from her. Thus, if Keith Campbell and I are correct, it would seem that a person could not travel back in time and meet herself. This would also entail that time travel is not possible.

Since I am committed to tropes, but find the notion of time travel fascinating, it would be nice if there was a way to reconcile trope theory with time travel. Perhaps there is a way of doing this.

According to modern physics, which is based on Einstein's special theory of relativity, there is no such thing as absolute and universal time. Instead, time is seen as being relative to each thing. In this context, time is relative in the sense that each thing carries around its own personal timescale which does not, in general, agree with the timescale of other entities. The relativity of time is subject to empirical proof. For example, if one precision atomic clock is left on earth and another is placed into the American space shuttle, the clock in the shuttle orbiting the earth will lag behind the clock left on earth. The difference in time is due to the speed of the shuttle and its location in earth's gravity well. Given the fact that this experiment has been conducted, it is hard to deny the relativity of time.

Once relativity is established, the notion of same time goes out the window. Each thing has it own timescale which varies with its location and speed, so there simply is no objective basis upon which sameness of time can be grounded. In this case, nothing can be in two different locations at the same time. Roughly put, being in a different location would put it in a different time.

One effect of the relativity of time would seem to be the end of instantiated universals. This is because an instantiated universal has to exist in different places at the same time. Since there is no such thing as sameness of time, instantiated universals simply cannot exist as defined.

A second effect of the relativity of time is that it enables time travel to be reconciled with tropes. The way this happens is as follows.

It is contended that people can be made of tropes, yet still be able to travel back in time to meet themselves. For example, imagine that Bill has travelled back in time to ask himself where he left his keys.

Bill tells future Bill where they are in return for a bit of advice on how to play the ponies later on. Both Bill and future Bill can be composed of identical tropes, yet still meet. This is possible because Bill and future Bill, like any other entities, will actually exist at different times. Hence, there is no need for Bill and future Bill to exist at the same time. They simply have to have their times 'close enough' to allow them to interact. Thus, I can have my tropes and time travel, too.

No chance for chance

Matters of chance, such as the roll of a die, are such a common part of life that almost everyone believes in random chance. Despite being widespread, this belief is not justified. This will be shown by drawing an analogy with David Hume's classic discussion of causation.[35]

Before exposure to philosophy, most people believe in causation. Seeing a billiard ball striking and apparently moving another ball, we think we have witnessed causation. But we do not observe causation. All we observe is event X followed by event Y. According to Hume, if we observe enough instances of X following Y, we begin to expect that X will always follow Y (think of Pavlov's Dog). However, regardless of the number of observations, we are not justified in our belief. When we say that X causes Y, we are reporting a psychological claim that we expect Y when we observe X. A similar case can be made for chance.

As with causation, most people believe in chance. We see dice roll and think the result will be a matter of chance. We do not, however, see chance – we just see the dice roll and land. There seem to be two 'reasons' for believing that chance is involved.

First, we tend to attribute chance to matters that are unpredictable. For example, when a die is rolled we know some number between one and six will result, but we do not know which. Because we cannot predict the outcome, we come to believe that chance must be involved.

While this helps explain the psychology of the belief, there are many things that are unpredictable that are not matters of chance.

For example, the effects of mixing two new chemicals together might be unpredictable (we won't know until we try), yet not a matter of chance. Saying that something is unpredictable simply reports our ignorance – it does not reveal the nature of chance.

A second way of looking at chance is to take something to be a matter of chance if things could have turned out differently. The rolling of a die seems to be an example of this. Though we rolled a three, we could have rolled a six. Having seen sixes rolled before, we come to believe things could have been different and thus believe that chance was involved. However, chance seems to be more than the possibility that things could have been different. After all, things could turn out differently in non-chance situations. For example, though we placed five kilograms of wheat on a scale, we could have placed ten kilograms. However, this would not be a matter of chance. Thus, chance seems to involve something more.

This something more seems to be that things could have been different, even if everything was identical to the original event. For example, suppose a person rolled a three on a die. If the situation was re-created perfectly and a six were rolled, then the only reasonable explanation would be that chance was involved.

Unfortunately, there is one flaw with this – we cannot perfectly re-create the events. In the case of the tossing of a die, this is obvious – no person could hold and throw the die exactly the same way twice in a row. And, of course, there would be other factors such as air currents, the rotation of the earth, the temperature of the die, the effect of the original throw on the die, and so on. Despite these problems, it might be thought the conditions could be re-created perfectly through various means (an incredibly precise robot arm in place of a person, etc.). However, there is one factor that could never be duplicated – time. Re-creating the event will be just that – a re-creation. If the die comes up three on the first roll and six on the second, this does not show that it could have been a six the first time. All its shows is that it was three the first time and six the second.

Of course, a possibility remains open – we could travel back in time and witness the event again. If things turn out differently, then perhaps we could conclude that we have at last found evidence of chance. But, of course, we would need to consider the fact that what changed the outcome was not chance but our presence in the past.

If we are willing to consider something even stranger than time travel, another possibility remains: parallel worlds. Some philosophers and scientists claim that there are worlds just like ours 'out there'. Thus, to prove that chance is real, we would just need to find evidence of a parallel world exactly like ours in which, using the die example, the die came up some number other than three on the first roll. Unfortunately, this would not help: the die roll in the parallel world would not be identical to the first die roll in our world. For the rolls to be identical, the worlds would need to be identical. But in that case we would have just one world, not two.

Thus, our belief in chance, like our belief in causation, seems to be based in our psychology and not on any firm foundation. Chance never had a chance.

The implausible secret

While positive thinking books are nothing new, Australian TV producer Rhonda Byrne has recently had a significant success with her books and DVD about 'the secret'.[36]This secret is what she calls 'the law of attraction'. This law states that reality can be altered and manipulated directly by people's thoughts and feelings. To use one of Byrne's own causal examples, 'food is not responsible for putting on weight. It is your thought that food is responsible for putting on weight that actually has food put on weight.'[37] She even claims that she can eat whatever she wants and maintain her weight.

The law of attraction also allegedly helps people acquire material goods. The film[38] shows a woman acquire a necklace and a boy get a bike, merely by visualizing the object of their desire.

This law apparently even helps with parking: in the film a financial consultant is able to find empty parking spaces by visualizing what he wants. While getting material goods and parking spaces is appealing, using this law can apparently also cure disease. For example, a woman in the film claims that she cured her breast cancer by positive thinking.

As one might suspect from these claims, the work puts forth a causal account that is both implausible and contrary to empirical evidence.

First, the claim that the law of attraction enables people to get what they want by their thoughts and feelings is contrary to the empirical evidence. For example, consider the Playstation 3. On the day of its initial release, many people wanted a PS3 very badly – badly enough to wait for hours and hours in line for a chance to get one. However, most of these people went home empty-handed. If the law of attraction worked, one would expect that there would be many more PS3 owners. As another example, consider grades. As a professor, I have lost count of the number of students who have told me how badly they want an 'A' and how focused they are on the grade. However, they are graded on the quality of their work and not once has an 'A' miraculously appeared in the grade book simply because a student wanted it badly enough. As a final example, consider illness. I, like many people, have had close friends who have had cancer and who maintained a positive attitude throughout the ordeal and wanted, very badly, to be healthy and to live. Unfortunately, this attitude is clearly not enough since death all too often puts an end to hope. Given that the law of attraction is contrary to experience, it seems reasonable to reject it as yet another form of wishful thinking.

Second, consider the specific examples used by Byrne. These examples run contrary to well-established and extensively tested scientific findings. Take, for example, her claim about food and weight. The physiological process of fat production in humans is well understood and well tested. It works in purely physical terms and there is simply no evidence that how people think about their food can affect the physiological process of fat production. After all, people in persistent vegetative states gain weight from food even though they presumably have no thoughts about food whatsoever. As another example, consider the claim made about cancer. While a person's attitude does have an impact on his or her health, there is no evidence that this attitude can actually cure cancer. While cancer is not as well understood as fat production, there is adequate understanding to effectively support the claim that cancer is a physiological phenomenon that is not curable simply by thoughts and feelings. Finally, consider the parking space example. If visualizing a space results in an empty space, this would seem to entail that people have great mental powers. To be specific, this would entail that people have the power to cause other people to avoid or leave a parking space simply by thinking. While extensive testing has been done on psychic phenomena, there is no adequate evidence that people have such powers.

Interestingly enough, these examples provide grounds for empirically testing the law of attraction via controlled experiments. For example, the alleged weight-control powers of the law of attraction could be tested by conducting a controlled experiment. In this experiment two groups of people would consume the same foods and engage in the same activities. The people in the experimental group would do their very best to think that food is not responsible for putting on weight. Those in the control group would not have that thought. Naturally, the subjects would have to be carefully observed (to keep people from, for example, eating less or exercising more). I contend that there would be no significant difference between the groups – but this is something that can (but probably will not) be tested.

In light of the weight of the evidence against and the lack of evidence for the law of attraction, it should be rejected on rational grounds. While a positive attitude is a good thing, to modify an old saying, 'If you want something done, you need to do it yourself.'

PART TWO:

ETHICS AND POLITICAL AND SOCIAL THOUGHT:

GOOD, EVIL, POLITICS AND ALL THAT STUFF

6 Gender and Ethics

While this section includes a discussion of pornography, there are no naughty pictures here. Instead you will find some very interesting, yet family-safe, articles about gender and related issues, such as same-sex marriage.

Of gender and numbers in academics and athletics

In 1972 the United States enacted Title IX. It states: 'No person in the United States shall, on the basis of sex, be excluded from participation in, be denied the benefits of, or be subject to discrimination under any education program or activity receiving federal assistance.'[39] This law was created to rectify the wrongful gender-based exclusion of women from activities. It obviously rests on the moral principle that exclusion and discrimination based on sex is wrong.

In 1993, it was decided Title IX[40] would be applied using more rigid standards. One new standard required schools to ensure that their athletic teams perfectly mirrored the gender distribution of the general student body. No other factor, such as the amount of interest in a sport, was to be considered. Not surprisingly, many feminists lauded these efforts to bring about gender equality. These efforts had two major effects. First, schools that could not create and fill new teams for women were forced to cut men's teams to balance the numbers. Second, schools that could not encourage enough women to join existing teams were forced to cut men until the proper numbers were reached. To put it bluntly, a male student could be denied the opportunity to participate in sports not because of a lack of determination or ability, but simply because he happened to be male. This clearly violates the letter of the law as well as the underlying moral principle regarding the immorality of gender-based exclusion. It is indeed ironic that a law intended to protect women from exclusion was used to exclude men.

Oddly enough, the feminists who fought against the exclusion of women are rather silent about this new exclusion. However, perhaps the moral principles these feminists follow do not include the principle that exclusion is wrong. Perhaps their true principle is that we are obligated to bring about numerical gender equality even at the cost of exclusion.

If this is their true principle, then it becomes difficult to explain the general lack of concern over the significant gender inequalities within the academic realm. Women compose 51 per cent of the population. But women make up 58 per cent of the student body and 61 per cent of the graduates of American community colleges. In 2002, for every 100 men who received a bachelor's degree there were 133 women. In the same year, for every 100 men who received a master's degree there were 138 women. Men, however, still outnumber women in the number of doctorates received.[41]

The situation is even more extreme for minorities. For every 100 African-American males earning a bachelor's degree there are 192 African-American women. The proportions are roughly the same for Hispanics and Native Americans.

Despite the glaring lack of gender equality, only a very few, such as Andy Sum of Northeastern University, Jessica Gavora, author of *Tilting the Playing Field*,[42] and Christina Hoff Sommers, author of *The War Against Boys*,[43] have raised concerns.

If the feminists were actually following a principle of numerical gender equality, then they would be obligated to insist that these numbers be balanced. As in the case of athletics, this would need to be done by requiring an increase in male enrolment. Schools that could not bring the number of men on a par with the number of women would, of course, be required to cut female students until equality was achieved.

Since feminists have largely failed to step forward and insist on the same numerical equality in academics as they expect in athletics, it is unlikely that they accept a principle of gender equality. Instead, it seems they must endorse a gender-biased principle or principles. Whatever specific principle(s) they follow, the principle(s) must include the following. First, gender inequality is unacceptable if it is tilted in favour of men. Second, it is acceptable to exclude men to bring about gender equality in an area. Third, gender inequality is acceptable if it is tilted in favour of women.

It certainly seems that any principle based on the above would violate the principle of relevant difference. This is the principle that it is only acceptable to treat two people or things differently if there is a relevant difference between them. In terms of athletics and academics, being a man or a woman does not seem to make a person more or less entitled to equal opportunity. Thus, it seems that it would be morally best to return to the original spirit of Title IX and insist that no one should be denied the opportunity to participate merely because of his or her gender.

Bad Girls

Once upon a time, little girls were said to be made of sugar, spice and everything nice. Times have changed.[44] The period 1980–2003 saw a 96 per cent increase in the number of girls (aged 10–17) being arrested for aggravated assault in the United States. In contrast, there was only a 13 per cent increase for boys. From 1983 to 2003 the number of girls arrested on weapon possession charges increased 125 per cent. For boys, the increase was 22 per cent. Girls are still lagging behind boys in terms of overall numbers – for every three boys arrested for violent crimes there is only one girl being arrested. But girls are apparently edging out boys in the number of schoolyard fights. These statistics, to steal an advertising phrase, show that 'you've come a long way, baby'.

Since this increase in crime and violence is undesirable, it is important to determine why it is happening. Given that the violent behaviour of both sexes is increasing, it is reasonable to suspect that there are common factors influencing both. The usual suspects can be trotted out in a line-up: the corruptive effects of the media, declining family values, poor role models, and so on. However, given that the effect on girls has been significantly greater, it seems equally reasonable to consider the possibility that there is a factor or factors that is either affecting them alone or affecting them to a far greater degree.

One plausible, if vague, candidate is the women's movement and feminism. Prior to the women's movement gaining momentum, the social norms called for males to be properly aggressive and females to be suitably restrained. The women's movement and feminism called for equality and encouraged women to become empowered.

On the face of it equality and empowerment seem like good things. Inequality, by its very nature, seems to imply unfairness and perhaps even injustice. Being underpowered would seem to involve weakness and vulnerability, plus the inability to accomplish things. However, the possibility that equality and empowerment have a dark side should be taken seriously.

First, consider the nature of equality. While the concept of equality comes in more varieties than Baskin Robbins ice cream,[45] the basic idea is that the women's movement aimed at making male and female situations more on a par. One side-effect of this process is that it seems to have made women more like men. After all, females now occupy various professional, private and social roles once occupied solely by males. For example, violent sports were once the domain of males but are now open to females. As another example, violent role models (such as action heroes) were once all male and now there are females in these roles. Given that these social roles help shape a person and her behaviour, it should be no surprise that females are acting more like males in negative ways as well. It would certainly be odd if taking on male roles only had a positive effect on females and that they somehow escaped the negative aspects.

Second, consider the nature of empowerment. For the most part, empowerment is about giving females power – presumably power equivalent to that held by males. The idea seems to be that empowerment would give females more freedom and make them less likely to become victims of male power. While freedom and strength can be good things, there seem to be two unfortunate aspects to most forms of empowerment.

The first unfortunate aspect is that for the most part discussions of empowerment seem to be devoid of discussion of ethics. There is a great deal of talk about empowering people, but little discussion about moral responsibility for that power and what sort of things a good person should do with that power. Simply empowering people without providing moral guides is very much like handing a person a gun or the keys to a car without giving them any suitable training. In the case of guns and cars, people will get hurt. Apparently the same holds true in the case of empowerment.

The second unfortunate aspect is that the empowerment of females often seems to involve encouraging them to adopt the aggressive traits of thought and behaviour traditionally encouraged in males. Given that these aggressive traits lead males to behave badly, it should be no surprise that these traits would also lead females to behave badly.

Since the women's movement has aimed at bringing about equality and empowerment for females and not males, this would help explain the difference in the increase in negative behaviour. While both males and females are affected by general factors that lead to violent behaviour, mostly or only females are affected by the aspects of the women's movement that aims at equality and empowerment. So, just as females are making increasing advances in other aspects of society (such as in jobs) they are also making increasing 'advances' in violence and crime.

It is important to note that the women's movement has been largely positive and that the negative side-effects should not be taken as justifying rolling back the progress that has been made by the movement. However, the increase in violence and crime among girls should be taken as a serious sign that we need to rethink what we are trying to achieve with equality and empowerment.

The Female Brain

In her book *The Female Brain* neuropsychiatrist Louann Brizendine[46] examines the biology that is supposed to lie behind gender differences.

In this work she examines such matters as why girls prefer dolls to trucks and the role of hormones in teenagers' obsession with text messaging and shopping. She also examines why women think about sex less than men think about it and why women might be having more affairs than before.

Not surprisingly, her work has many critics. The main criticisms take two forms. The first is that such a work is rather pointless because gender differences are insignificant. The second is that her work is likely to have a negative impact by undermining women and reinforcing existing gender stereotypes.

Janet Hyde, a psychologist, has been very critical of the work.[47] She did an analysis of studies comparing the emotions and behaviours of men and women and she claimed to find that the gender differences are not statistically significant. From this she concluded that there are really no gender differences to explain.

However, Hyde's conclusion seems to be false. A look at the United States' education system reveals that there are some very significant differences in behaviour. Males currently make up 70 per cent of those classified as having learning disabilities, 80 per cent of those who drop out of high school and only 45 per cent of those enrolled in higher education. As stated earlier, for every 100 men in 2002 who received a bachelor's degree there were 133 women. In the same year, for every 100 men who received a master's degree there were 138 women.[48] Additional clear examples of significant differences in behaviour can also be found in the number and types of crimes committed by members of each gender as well as their participation in various leisure activities, such as video games. While these are behavioural examples, they most likely also indicate differences in emotional makeup as well.

In addition to the behavioural evidence, there are also physiological reasons to believe that women are different from men. Women differ from men in levels of oestrogen, cortisol and dopamine and these would certainly seem to have some impact on emotions and behaviour. Women also have 11 per cent more neurons devoted to emotions and memory. This also seems to indicate there would be a difference between men and women in terms of emotions and behaviour. After all, it seems quite reasonable to believe there is a connection between physiology, emotions and behaviour.

Of course, it is also possible that these physiological differences are not enough to really be significant in terms of behaviour and emotions. If this is the case, then an alternative explanation would be needed for the differences in behaviour – such as the significant differences between men and women in education.

One stock alternative explanation is that differences are the result of nurture and not nature. For example, Psychiatrist Nancy C. Andreason claims that nurture is the decisive factor and that the measurable differences 'are used to oppress and suppress women'.[49]

Her claim is interesting in that it seems to run against the claim made by Hyde that the differences between the emotions and behaviour of the genders are not statistically significant. After all, if nurture is creating measurable differences between the genders that can be exploited to oppress and suppress women, then it would seem likely that they are statistically significant. Her claim is also interesting in that it adds a moral element to the matter at hand – namely that the differences are wrongly used to harm women.

Since humans have to rely so much on learning (as opposed to instinct) it seems quite reasonable to believe that nurture has a significant effect on creating at least some gender differences in behaviour and emotions. However, for the reasons given above, it also seems equally reasonable to conclude that physiology also plays a role in some of the differences.

Regardless of their basis, it is well worth being concerned about how differences between the genders might be used or misused. As has been pointed out, these alleged differences have often been used to attempt to justify the oppression of women. Given this fact, moral arguments can be presented as to why works that present or explain such differences should be opposed. Ironically, such moral arguments would raise other moral concerns about restricting the search for truth.

There are other moral concerns as well. One moral concern is based on the possibility that men and women are different enough for this to have significance in the field of medicine. It is quite obvious that men and women have different physiologies and that these have medical significance in terms of health risks, diseases and treatment. For example, men do not get pregnant, nor do they undergo menopause. As another example, women obviously do not get prostrate cancer and do not suffer from erectile dysfunction. Given such differences, it is reasonable and medically sound to treat men and women differently in such cases. Not to take into account such medically relevant differences would be irresponsible and potentially harmful.

In light of the medically relevant physiological differences it seems reasonable to consider the possibility that men and women differ in ways relevant to psychiatric medicine and psychological treatment. It would be wrong and irresponsible simply to assume otherwise or to ignore such differences for 'political' reasons. As such, the sort of research conducted by Brizendine is worth conducting. If differences are found, then this information should be used to help women and certainly not to oppress or suppress them. Naturally, it might turn out that the differences are not significant – but that is something that should be determined scientifically.

Gender segregation in education

Plato argued for gender equality in education[50] but his vision remained unrealized for centuries. After a long struggle for gender integration in education, the debate has reignited and arguments are being made in favour of gender-segregated education.

Two plausible arguments in favour of educational segregation are as follows.

First is the physiology argument. Recent studies indicate differences exist that are potentially relevant to education. For example, males supposedly do better on timed multiple-choice tests because their testosterone levels make them more competitive.

Assuming such differences exist, segregation would be justified by the principle of relevant difference: it is morally acceptable to treat people differently if their differences justify such treatment.

To use an analogy, consider medicine. Males and females, as we have observed, are physically different in many medically relevant respects. Now, imagine there are three drugs for treating an illness. The first does a mediocre job of treating males and females, the second works very well for males but poorly for females, and the third works the other way around. Given that consequences matter, it would be acceptable, even preferable, to use the gender-specific drugs rather than providing only the mediocre drug to everyone.

If this analogy holds, then educational segregation based on relevant differences would be as morally justified as the use of the hypothetical medicines.

Second, there is the empirical evidence argument. Studies show that such segregation can result in educational improvements. As an example, the Foust Elementary school in Kentucky implemented such programmes and found improvements in test scores and a decrease in behavioural problems.

Further, males are doing poorly in the existing education system. In the United States, males currently make up 70 per cent of those classified as having learning disabilities, 80 per cent of those who drop out of high school and only 45 per cent of those enrolled in higher education. This is taken as evidence for gender bias in the current system.[51]

Finally, there is significant anecdotal support. For example, many women who attended segregated institutions contend that their education was improved by not having to expend time and concern on being appealing to males and the absence of the disruptive and intimidating behaviour of males.

If this information is correct, a utilitarian argument can be given in favour of segregated education: integrated education creates significant harms – as shown by the statistics regarding males. Segregated education has been shown to provide significant benefits in education. Assuming that harms are morally undesirable and benefits are morally desirable, gender segregation in education seems acceptable – even laudable.

Further, if males are currently doing worse than females in education because of a gender bias, then many of the arguments previously employed by feminists supporting changes aimed at making things better for females can easily be refurbished and employed to support segregation in education. Segregation would permit each gender to get the maximum benefit from education and everyone would be better off.

Although these are reasonable arguments in favour of gender segregation in education, there are some equally reasonable concerns.

One reasonable moral concern is that history has shown that segregation tends to lead to situations that are separate but unequal. Gender-segregated education could lead to such a situation. One reason is as follows. Feminists contend that women have less power and wealth than men. Combining this with the fact that people tend to use their power and wealth to benefit their own kind, it seems reasonable to suspect that education for females would suffer relative to education for males.

A second reason is that given the current state of education for males, one might suspect that women have the most power and influence in the education system. Given that people tend to use their power and their influence for their own benefit, it seems reasonable to suspect that education for males would continue to suffer relative to education for females.

Either way, it seems likely that one gender will be short-changed – this is the normal course of events in attempts to create separate but equal systems. Hence, this is a reasonable moral concern.

A final concern relates to the goals of education. If the only goal is to educate efficiently, then segregated education seems reasonable. However, public education also aims at instilling social values. In the Western democracies, this involves teaching the value of diversity and furthering social integration. If males and females are placed in separate educational systems, it seems reasonable to believe that this could exacerbate existing problems between the genders and perhaps create new ones. The similarities to racial segregation seem obvious and provide good grounds for being concerned with gender segregation in education.

Porn and princes

Feminists have long been concerned with the way women are portrayed in various forms of media, ranging from advertisements to pornography. In general, feminists have claimed that women are all too often portrayed, in varying degrees, as mere sex objects and not as full human beings. This is wrong, they argue, because it objectifies women and encourages men to treat them as things rather than people.

A recent variation on this argument focuses on cases in which attractive women are presented as highly sexual beings. In short, women are portrayed as sex goddesses. Obvious examples include soft pornography magazines such as *Maxim* and *Playboy* as well as racier material such as *Penthouse* and internet pornography.

This argument, put simply, is that such presentations are psychologically harmful to women and men because they create unrealistic expectations. Naturally, the harms are different for men and women.

In the case of women, such portrayals are wrong because they provide unrealistic standards of beauty and behaviour. The harm occurs when women judge themselves against these standards and find themselves lacking, thus potentially suffering harm to their self-esteem.

Even more pernicious is the fact that the standards go beyond being unrealistic – they are all but impossible to meet. When a woman is portrayed in *Maxim* or *Playboy* she has already been selected as being considerably more attractive than average. Further, she also benefits from the assistance of others, such as personal trainers, makeup artists, and professional photographers who do their best to make her appear beautiful. Finally, her image is enhanced by the use of either traditional airbrush techniques or with software such as Adobe Photoshop. As an analogy to show the near impossibility of meeting the standards, imagine that being attractive is like placing well in a five kilometre foot race. Now imagine that a number of Olympic-quality runners are selected and carefully prepared for this race. They, unlike the other competitors, are given racing bikes to use in the race. Now imagine that all other runners are compared to them and are looked down upon when they fail to be as fast.

In the case of men, it is claimed that viewing such images gives them unrealistic expectations of how women should look and behave. While this is alleged to create a variety of harms, a primary problem is the creation of dissatisfaction. Specifically, a man under the influence of such expectations can become dissatisfied with his partner and this can spell disaster for the relationship. For example, a man who, so influenced, becomes dissatisfied with his wife's appearance and sexual appetite might start ignoring her or might stray into adultery.

This scenario is quite plausible and nicely parallels the way consumer dissatisfaction is created in advertising: consumers are shown products that are (alleged to be) better than their current products, thus leading them to replace the old products with new products. The parallels between the ways women are presented in the media and the ways products are advertised is rather obvious. Hence the similarity in effects is to be expected.

While women are portrayed as attractive and very sexual beings in order to appeal to male fantasies, men are also portrayed in ways that appeal to female fantasies. While men are not portrayed in the same manner as women, such portrayals create unrealistic expectations about men in terms of how they should look and how they should behave.

Obvious examples include women's magazines and romantic films, such as *Titanic*, which present the masculine ideal in terms of such things as being handsome, romantic, and devoted to one's love to the point of utter self-sacrifice (like dying in the cold waters of the Atlantic). In short, the ideal man is presented as, to use the stock phrase, a Prince Charming.

Given the above discussion, it is reasonable to think that if harm arises from the portrayal of women as sex goddesses, then harm also arises from portraying men as Prince Charmings. Naturally, the harms are different for men and women.

In the case of men, it is contended that such portrayals are wrong because they provide unrealistic standards of male beauty. The harm occurs when men judge themselves against these standards and find themselves lacking, thus potentially suffering harm to their self-esteem. In all honesty, men are less likely to suffer from this than women, but it is still a matter of concern.

In the case of women, they can develop unrealistic expectations of how men should look and behave. While a variety of problems might arise from this, the main problem is the creation of dissatisfaction. To be specific, a woman under the influence of such expectations will become dissatisfied with her partner and this will spell disaster for the relationship in some manner. For example, a woman might expect her partner to give her regular gifts of flowers 'just to show he cares', sing serenades to her, maintain a 'six pack' (abs not beer) and express his feelings for her with deep, poetic sensitivity. Since most males are not up to such things, the woman might grow cold and distant or seek solace in the arms of another.

Given the well-published statistics regarding divorces and affairs and the fact that entire industries are springing up to assist the faithless in said affairs, it seems reasonable to believe there is a great deal of dissatisfaction among men and women. It also seems reasonable to believe that the way men and women are portrayed plays a role in this dissatisfaction. One way to solve the problem is for men and women to try to live up to the expectations. However, feminists have argued quite effectively that it would be morally wrong to expect women to live up to such unrealistic standards of beauty and sexuality. The generally proposed solution to such problems is to change the portrayals of women to be more realistic or possibly eliminating certain types of portrayals altogether, such as those in pornography. This seems quite reasonable, assuming that the alleged harms are real. Of course, if this is done for women, the principle of consistent application (that a moral standard must be applied consistently) requires that the same be done for men. Thus it would seem that one of the secrets for a successful relationship might well be lowering one's expectations until they are met.

The morality of same-sex marriage

While the issue of same-sex marriage has been debated for some time, recent events have brought it into the spotlight. Not surprisingly, this issue stirs up strong feelings and these sometimes get expressed as coherent arguments. This provocation will address some of the arguments aimed at showing same-sex marriage is immoral or should at least not be morally permissible.

One of the most popular arguments against same-sex marriage is that it is immoral because it is forbidden by God. This argument is based in what philosophers call divine command theory, which is the view that morality is defined by God's commands.

Despite its popularity, this argument suffers from serious problems. Laying aside the difficulty of proving that God exists, there is the question of determining what God actually permits and forbids. While some churches hold that God forbids same-sex marriage, others disagree and are willing to perform such ceremonies. The heart of the problem is that there does not seem to be any objective and reliable way to discern which church (if any) has God's view right. Hence, this argument provides no grounds for concluding that same-sex marriage is immoral.

A second problem can be shown by the following analogy: I make rules for my pets ('thou shall not scratch my leather chair with thy claws') and the rules define good and bad behaviour. Since rules that are not enforced are meaningless and my pets are weaker than me, they can only do wrong in secret or very quickly (before I can stop them). Since God is omniscient and presumably very quick, no one should be able actually to break his rules. Hence, if God truly forbids same-sex marriages, they would never occur.

It might be objected that God forbids same-sex marriages and though he does nothing on earth to enforce his rules, he punishes rule-breakers later with hell. In reply, this would be analogous to me making the 'no scratching' rule, letting the cats merrily scratch the hell out of my chair at will, and then punishing the cats years later by soaking them in gasoline and setting them ablaze. If I did such a thing, I would justly be seen as a cruel, vicious and evil person. Surely God is not cruel, vicious or evil and if he did not want same-sex marriage to take place, he would stop it before he had to punish beings infinitely weaker than him.

Given the problems with the religious argument, opponents of same-sex marriage also employ non-religious moral arguments.

One common argument is that the purpose of marriage is to produce children. Obviously, same-sex couples cannot produce children. Hence, same-sex marriage should not be permitted.

The obvious problem with this argument is that many 'different sex' marriages do not produce children, either because the couples cannot or decide not to have them. Given the above argument, such couples should not be morally permitted to marry. Since this is absurd, the argument should be rejected. Further, advances in technology will almost certainly permit same-sex couples to produce children of their own. When such technology becomes a reality, the argument would be completely undercut.

A second common argument is that homosexuals are immoral and hence they should not be morally permitted to marry.

One flaw in this argument is that homosexuals do not seem to be any more or any less immoral than heterosexuals. For example, homosexuals do not seem to be any more inclined to lie, cheat, steal or commit murder than heterosexuals. Hence, there seems to be no more reason to reject same-sex marriages than traditional marriages on these grounds.

It might be objected that being homosexual is itself immoral and hence same-sex marriage should be prevented on moral grounds.

In reply, moral consistency requires that the principle 'immoral people should not marry' should be applied across the board. This would entail that immoral heterosexuals should also not be morally permitted to marry. If taken seriously, this would mean that prospective couples would need to submit to a moral evaluation before being granted a licence.

While the notion of preventing immoral people from marrying (and reproducing) has a certain appeal, there do not seem to be any moral grounds for denying bad people the right to marry. This, of course, assumes that the marriage is not otherwise morally questionable – such as a forced marriage or a marriage that is part of a scam or swindle.

A third argument is that same-sex marriage will undermine traditional values and yield dire, yet vague, consequences. Because of these harms, same-sex marriage should not be morally permitted.

There are two replies to this argument. First, married heterosexuals have done such a good job acting against 'traditional values' that it seems unlikely that permitting same-sex marriages could possible do any more damage. After all, it is hard to imagine that homosexuals would engage in more adultery and spousal abuse than heterosexuals.

Second, it is not clear exactly what new harms will arise or what old harms will increase if same-sex marriage is permitted. For example, it seems very unlikely that permitting same-sex marriage will increase child abuse, theft, murder, war, rape, or genocide.

Perhaps the only compelling argument against it is that as long as same-sex marriage is not permitted, homosexuals are protected from the costs of weddings, adultery and divorce.

7   Technology and Ethics

While technology is fascinating, the associated moral issues raised by such things as RFID, genetic engineering, gender selection and virtual violence in video games are perhaps even more interesting.

Evil spam

Anyone who has an email account is familiar with spam – the unwanted, unasked-for email that typically offers, among other things, dubious products, pyramid schemes, scams and pornography. Laying aside moral questions about the content of spam, there is the question of the morality of spam itself.

The few spammers who are willing to discuss it claim that advertising spam is acceptable. Typically, they argue their spam is like any form of advertising. They often draw an analogy between spam and printed mail advertising. If pressed further, they tend to assert they have a right to make money.

It is contended that the practice of spamming is immoral. To prove this, I will address the standard defence of spam.

The analogy between spam and postal advertising is a false one. In the case of postal advertising, the advertiser has to pay postage. With spam, the spammer pays nothing for the spam she sends. Sticking with the analogy, the spammer is like a person who sneaks bags of advertising into the mail trucks without paying the postage.

The spammer might reply that she, like everyone else, pays her ISP a monthly fee and this entitles her to send out the spam. To counter this, an analogy can be drawn with a toll-highway. Each person who pays the toll has the right to take his vehicle on to the highway. The spammer is like a person who thinks that since he paid the toll, he has the right to bring a convoy of tractor trailers on to the highway. Given that a spammer will send thousands of emails at a time, it is reasonable to claim that his use (abuse) of the system exceeds what he has paid for. Thus, spamming is wrong. If the spammers paid their fair share, then their advertising would be like postal advertising and just as acceptable.

The 'right to make money' is a common defence and has been used by everybody from honest business people to members of drug cartels. While it is not clear if there is such a right, let it be assumed for the sake of argument.

Even if there is a right to make money, there is still a hierarchy of rights – some rights are more important than others. For example, the right to free speech is outweighed by the right not to be harmed. Thus, I do not have the right to yell 'he's got SARs' in a crowded theatre.

In the case of the spammer's 'right' to make money, the main question is: do her spamming activities violate the rights of others?

If people have a right to make money, it also seems reasonable to grant them other rights, such as the right not to be annoyed and the right not to have their time wasted. While it can be difficult to judge rights, it seems reasonable that another person's right to make money does not give him the right to annoy others and waste their time.

Spam tends to be annoying to most people. Although there are programs that help filter spam, separating the spam from the non-spam and getting rid of the spam still wastes time. Thus, spam seems to violate people's rights and is hence immoral.

The spammer can reply that the annoyance and lost time is rather small for each individual – a minute or two per day. Surely, she would say, her right to make money outweighs such minor inconveniences.

When making this reply, the spammer is taking the harm to be non-cumulative. As she sees it, she is only doing a little bit of harm to each person, so she concludes she is doing only a very little harm. However, this line of reasoning is flawed. If a person steals $1 from one person, she has stolen just a little money. But, if she steals $1 each from one million people, she has not stolen a little bit of money – she has stolen quite a lot. In the case of spam, the spammer is like the thief – she has not taken much from each, but he has taken much from the whole. Given that spammers send massive amounts of emails, the time they waste and the annoyance they generate is truly staggering. Given the substantial amount of harm they are creating, it must be concluded that spam is immoral, even assuming people have a right to make money.

The spammers can address this by putting in their subject header the word 'spam'. This way people who do not wish to have their time wasted can simply set their email filters to block all spam. Those who wish to receive spam can simply leave their inboxes undefended. Thus, the spammers can act on their right to make money and everyone else can exercise their right not to be annoyed and not have their time wasted.

The neutral net

We are currently living in a golden age of internet equality and democracy. To be specific, under the current system all data is generally treated equally. Because of this you can access a teenager's blog on Paris Hilton as quickly as you can access the *New York Times* website. However, as with all previous golden ages, this one's days are numbered.

Currently some internet service providers (ISPs) use software and hardware to slow down large downloads and BitTorrent traffic.[52] But this is just the beginning. Major ISPs such as AT&T and Verizon are proposing a new model for the net. If the current model is a democracy, the new model will be a plutocracy: instead of all pages being treated equally, there will be a fee-based hierarchy in which one's status depends on what one can afford to pay for. Those who wish to provide rapid access to their sites or data will have to pay a premium. Sites that do not or cannot pay these premiums will still probably be accessible but at significantly slower rates. There are also rumours that some ISPs will be able to block access to their competitors' sites and services. For example, a phone company's ISP customers might find that their Skype connections no longer seem to work. Not surprisingly, these possibilities raise a variety of moral concerns.

A reasonable argument can easily be given in favour of the non-neutral net. To provide faster access the ISPs will have to acquire new hardware. Naturally, this hardware will not be free. Given the extra cost associated with providing the faster service, it seems quite reasonable for the ISPs to charge more for such premium services. To use an analogy, it is reasonable for a restaurant to charge customers more for meals with more expensive ingredients. It would be, for example, rather absurd for a customer to claim that she should get a lobster dinner for the same price as a bowl of chicken noodle soup.

A further argument can be given by drawing an analogy to television infomercials and commercials. Nearly anyone can have their material broadcast. But if they want it to be on a channel and time that people actually watch, then the person must expect to pay more. Similarly, people must expect to pay more if they want their internet material provided to their viewers at premium speeds.

Interestingly, the analogy to television presents a matter of concern in regards to the non-neutral net. Almost anyone can have their material broadcast on television provided that they meet two basic conditions. First, they can pay for the service. Second, the material is something that the owners of the media entity are willing to allow on the air.

Because the net is currently neutral, these two basic conditions do not apply to internet content. However, a non-neutral net, perhaps dubbed the 'biasnet', would likely create a situation analogous to that of television and other commercial media. Those wishing to provide content in a rapid manner would have to pay the requisite fees and might be subject to censorship in regards to content.

The concern about the cost might be countered by repeating the argument given above – it is fair and reasonable to charge people extra for a premium product. The concern about censorship can be countered by arguing that a non-neutral net does not entail censorship – the ISPs would simply charge more for premium services and not engage in such behaviour.

In regards to cost the main moral concern is not that people would be charged for premium services but that this process would create two nets: a premium net and a slower net. Those who can afford the fees would enjoy the benefits of the premium net and those who could not would be relegated to the slower net. This would create a division in the net that mirrors the economic division of society and would thus create yet one more realm of inequality and undo the potential of the neutral net.

One positive aspect of the neutral net is that it provides great potential for equality and democracy. To give a specific example, much has been said about how the net can change politics. On the old model, in order to get elected a politician needs access to the major media and this requires great wealth. This means that major elections are limited to the wealthy or those indebted to the wealthy. On the new model, a person of modest means could run a relatively cheap web campaign and perhaps even stand a chance of winning. However, a non-neutral net would return the game to the old playing field – only those with access to the requisite wealth would be able to use the premium net. Those without the requisite means would be relegated to the slower net (which would probably be regarded as a virtual slum or ghetto). If democracy and equality are good things, then it would seem that the neutral net should be preserved as a social good by democracies.

In regards to the matter of censorship, it can be argued that by its very nature a non-neutral net would involve censorship. Only the content of those who could pay would appear on the premium net. It could be argued that this is no different from the other media. This is quite true – but this merely shows that economic censorship is practised in those media.

It can also be argued that a premium net would be subject to censorship by drawing an analogy to other media. Censorship is rampant in the realm of television, newspapers and radio. Bleeping and blurring are common occurrences and, of course, the censorship is best shown by what does not appear in the media. It seems likely that the same practices would be extended to the net as the ISPs gain more control over it under the guise of providing premium services.

Given the above arguments, it seems that the neutral net is something that should be preserved – provided that equality, freedom and democracy are valuable. If we wish to create yet another realm of censorship and inequality we should by all means endorse the premium net.

V is for video game . . . and violence

The idea of limiting or censoring violent and sexual artistic works dates back at least to Plato's *Republic*. The latest attempts to limit such imitations of violence and sexuality are focused on one of the newest artistic mediums: video games.[53]

Not surprisingly, the United States is leading the charge against the corrupting effects of these video games. In 2002 Senator Joe Lieberman introduced a bill intended to make it a federal crime to sell violent games to minors. Since then at least 28 American states have attempted to pass laws limiting the sale of such games to minors. For example, the governor of Illinois recently signed a law that imposes fines of up to $1,000 on those selling violent or sexually explicit games to minors. Not to be outdone, the governor of California, Arnold Schwarzenegger, signed a similar bill. Presumably, the law does apply to video games based on his *Terminator* and *Predator* movies.

Hillary Clinton, a woman who knows a bit about sexual immorality, has made it a mission to combat the nefarious influence of Grand Theft Auto. She alleges that the game is robbing American youth of their innocence. The families of two Alabama police officers and a dispatcher most likely agree with Clinton. They allege that Devin Moore killed these three people because of Grand Theft Auto. Hence they are suing those involved in making and selling the game: Sony, Take-Two, Rockstar Games, GameStop and Walmart. They are also suing Devin Moore.

Not surprisingly, the video game situation raises a variety of interesting philosophical issues. One such issue is whether or not a democratic government should be engaged in placing such restrictions on an artistic medium. A reasonable argument can be given in support of the claim that such restrictions are morally acceptable and perhaps even commendable.

It is generally accepted that governments have a moral obligation to protect their citizens from harm. Intuitively, the citizens that are more vulnerable should be given more protection than the less vulnerable. Minors are typically regarded as being rather limited in their ability to make mature or wise decisions and this makes them more vulnerable to certain harms than adults. Because of this most governments have laws restricting their access to harmful things such as alcohol, automobiles, guns, tobacco and voting. If video games are harmful, then placing such restrictions makes moral sense. To use an analogy, just as minors should be protected from their poor judgement in regards to cancer causing tobacco, they should be protected from corrupting video games until they are old enough to (at least in theory) make an informed decision.

While the argument is reasonable, its success or failure largely rests on whether video games are harmful or not. After all, if they are not harmful, then there would be no reason to protect minors from them.

Over the years numerous attempts have been made to determine whether video games are harmful to minors or not. At this time the evidence for such games being harmful is, at best, inconclusive. This is hardly shocking when the matter of causal connections is suitably considered. Obviously, a person can be violent or sexually depraved without ever being exposed to video games. The history of the world prior to the rise of violent and sexually explicit games nicely establishes this. Equally obvious is the fact that people can be exposed to violent or sexually explicit games and not be affected. Since the advent of video games millions of people have played and are playing violent video games. If there was even an extremely small causal connection between video games and violent or sexually depraved behaviour, then one would expect a noticeable increase in such behaviour correlating with the increase in video gaming. Since there does not seem to have been any such relevant increase, it is reasonable to conclude that video games have little or no effect on such behaviour.

This reply can be countered by arguing that the harm inflicted by such video games is more subtle and that the children are being harmed in ways that are not immediately evident. As with cancer caused by smoking, these harms might take years to manifest themselves. Because of these potential subtle harms, it can be argued that video games should be controlled by the government.

A reply to this counter is that if the politicians are truly motivated by a desire to protect children from harm, then their energy and governmental resources would be better spent elsewhere. While video games might have some subtle harmful effects on children, it is obvious that things such as poverty, lack of healthcare and unequal educational opportunities have rather unsubtle harmful effects on children. Once these substantial problems have been dealt with, then perhaps governments will have the time to deal with the alleged dangers of video games.

Virtual violence and moral purpose

In the *Republic* Plato[54] presents an argument for censorship based on the claim that art appeals to the emotions and encourages people to give in to these emotions. Giving way to these emotions is undesirable because it can lead to shameful or even dangerous behaviour. Viewing tragic plays might lead a person to give in to self pity and behave poorly. Exposure to violent art might cause a person to yield more readily to the desire to commit violence. Plato's solution is to ban such art in order to prevent its corrupting influence.

In recent years, this sort of reasoning has been used to argue that violent video games should be banned or at least stamped with very stern warning labels. The general idea is that such games can, via their nefarious powers, have a corrupting influence that might result in undesirable behaviour.

While this argument has a certain appeal, for years I regarded it as unconvincing. My view was not based on any logical flaw in the argument but on my own experience. In games such as Marathon, Doom, Quake and Half-Life my friends and I wantonly (albeit virtually) slaughtered assorted foes by the untold thousands. Despite far too many hours spent in such practices I did not notice any detrimental effect on our characters. As far as I could tell, we still regarded real violence as, in general, a bad thing and continued to resolve disputes rationally. Thus, for years I confidently rejected Plato's argument . . . until a friend loaned me a copy of Grand Theft Auto III.

In this game you play, to put it mildly, a rather bad person. Like many video games, you play through a series of missions aimed at achieving various ends. Unlike most games, the missions involve rather unsavoury activities, such as clubbing a pimp to death or driving a hooker to the local clinic. You can strike off on your own and engage in such praiseworthy activities as stealing cars (including ambulances), mugging hookers, or running over pedestrians (with stolen vehicles). At one point in the game my pockets were bulging with stolen cash and I had at least four ambulances and three police cars burning in the streets. It was at that moment that I realized that Plato was at least partially right – I could actually feel the game's corrupting influence. I popped the disk out and never put it in again.

Being a hardcore gamer, this did not end my gaming days. After receiving Halo as a gift, I popped it in and, after a slight hesitation, got to work slaughtering aliens. Though virtual bodies were piling up around me, the feeling I had experienced from playing Grand Theft Auto III never returned.

As a philosopher, I was determined to find the basis for the difference between the two experiences. It obviously was not in the violence itself – Halo and the other games all involved killing on a truly monumental scale. Thinking further, I realized that the other games, the ones that had no effect on me, all had a clear moral purpose behind the violence. For example, in games like Doom, Quake and Half-Life you are fighting to save your own life and the human race against truly wicked opponents. In Halo, you are fighting to save humanity from the

Covenant – a group of aliens who are intent on exterminating human-ity. In Grand Theft Auto you are cast in the role of a bad person who is doing bad things for his own selfish ends.

To put it in Aristotelian terms,[55] in games like Halo one is acting in the right way towards the right persons for the right reasons. In games like Grand Theft Auto III, one is typically acting in the wrong way towards the wrong people for the wrong reasons. If this is correct, it is no surprise that games like Halo did not have a corrupt-ing influence – when playing them you can be acting in a virtually virtuous manner. It is also unsurprising that Grand Theft Auto III had a negative influence – when playing it you are acting in a virtu-ally vicious manner (appropriately enough, the sequel to the game is called Vice City).

Thus it is not the corrupting influence of violence that we should fear. Instead, what should be of concern is the moral purpose, or lack thereof, behind the violence.

This is your brain on video games

While real violence abounds in the world, researchers and politicians continue to devote some of their attention to the debate about the effects of the virtual violence of video games.

While much of the research on video games has focused on behav-ioural studies, researchers at Indiana University set out to determine the short-term physiological effects of such games on the brain. In the experiment, half the test subjects played a violent video game, specifi-cally the first-person shooter Medal of Honor: Frontline. The other half of the group played a non-violent, but exciting, automobile racing game. After the games ended, the participants' brains were scanned. Compared to those playing the racing game, those playing the violent game had greater activity in the areas of the brain associated with emo-tions. In the case of the prefrontal areas of the brain (which are asso-ciated with self-control, inhibition and focus) those playing the violent game had less activity than those playing the racing game.[56]

The experiment's results are hardly surprising. In the context of a first-person shooter, focus and inhibition are disadvantageous. Too much focus can impede awareness of the general situation and inhibitions can cause a person to hesitate when action is required. From an evolutionary standpoint it makes sense that humans have this response to violent contexts – if they did not, humans would have had a greatly reduced chance of survival in conflict situations such as in hunting and in battle.

Brad Bushman, a psychology professor at the University of Michigan, interpreted the results as showing that the brain states experienced by those playing violent video games cause people to make 'impulsive, bad choices' (K. Springen (2006), 'This is your brain on alien killer pimps of Nazi doom'. *Newsweek*, 11 December, 48). He further contends that violent media increase aggressive thoughts and infers violent video games would have a stronger impact than passive media.

In light of these results, some parents have decided that their children will no longer be allowed to play video games. Further, some people regard the experiment as providing evidence that can be used to justify restricting or censoring violent video games. This is, of course, only one of many possible responses to the findings.

While it might seem odd, the findings can actually be used to argue in favour of violent video games. The argument for this is as follows.

As many politicians continuously warn us and as the news constantly shows, the world is a violent and dangerous place. If violent video games condition and prepare people for violence, then those who play such games will be better equipped to handle this violent and dangerous world. Thus, children should not be deterred from playing these games – they should be encouraged to play them so as to be prepared to face the world. While it could be argued that it would make more sense to create a better and more peaceful real world, there somehow seems to be little will or inclination to do that.

The matter of war further bolsters this argument. As the situations in Iraq and Afghanistan continue to deteriorate and the war on terror escalates, it is evident that the West will need an ever-growing number of soldiers. Getting them mentally prepared through video games can have a very positive effect – they will be better prepared to face the violence and will already have experienced virtual combat. If today's children will be tomorrow's soldiers, then it would be good for them to be as prepared as possible for the wars they will be fighting. Thus, violent video games should be encouraged.

The connection between video games and war preparation is further supported by the fact that various militaries have developed video games for training purposes. The United States has even developed military video games for civilian distribution – presumably as a recruiting and training tool. In light of this, it seems that violent commercial games can be part of this recruitment and training process. Even better, in regards to the commercial video games, the potential soldiers start training early and at their own expense.

It could be argued that it would be better if the same resources and energy that were used to create wars were employed to bring about a better world in which conflict was resolved in a rational and peaceful manner. However, the leaders of the world seem quite devoted to war and enamoured of violence. Hence, it would seem to be a mistake to try to bring about a virtual peace in the realm ōf video games.

In light of the violent nature of the world and the almost certain need for more and more soldiers, it would seem that violent video games are acceptable and even desirable. After all, it makes little sense to focus on virtual peace when the world is awash with real war and violence.

A better brain

One of the goals of modern neuroscience is to develop ways to improve human cognitive abilities. Researchers are currently working on what are known as 'smart pills' – drugs intended to improve memory, concentration and other mental abilities. Not surprisingly, there is already significant ethical debate over such enhancements.

One type of enhancement aims at restoring capabilities that have been impaired or lost due to such things as injury, disease or ageing. For example, medications are being devised to offset the effects of Alzheimer's disease. These enhancements seem to be morally acceptable. Using medication to, for example, restore a patient's ailing memory is analogous to using surgery to repair bone damage or using antibiotics to restore a patient's physical health. Such 'traditional' treatments are morally acceptable; hence the use of enhancements for such purposes is equally acceptable.

Not surprisingly, the moral controversy centres on the use of enhancements to boost the mental capabilities of healthy people. Given that healthy people have used drugs, such as steroids, to enhance their physical abilities, it is safe to conclude that they will use products to boost their mental abilities.

While it is tempting to regard the use of such enhancers as immoral across the board, there are situations in which their use by healthy individuals would be acceptable. For example, a surgeon performing a long and complex life-saving procedure or rescue workers in a major disaster would certainly benefit from using a concentration booster to keep them alert and focused in their life-saving efforts. In such situations, the benefits of using them would outweigh potential harms, provided that the products did not have significant side-effects.

In other cases the use of such products would be immoral. The clearest and most obvious example would be using them to gain an edge in academics. For example, students would no doubt be tempted to use such enhancers to improve their scores on standardized admissions tests, like the LSAT and GRE. The immorality of such uses can be shown using the following analogy.

In competitive sports, such as running, the competition is governed by rules and the objective is to determine who is the best rather than who can win by any means. For example, if a person attempted to win a foot race by using an 'enhancement' like roller blades, a skateboard or a car, he would be rightfully regarded as doing something wrong. Using an enhancing drug, such as steroids, would be ethically on a par with using roller blades and, as such, would be morally unacceptable.

Assuming the goal of academic competitions, such as standardized tests, is to determine who is the best rather than who can achieve the highest score by any means, then it would follow that using mental enhancers to gain an edge would be analogous to using steroids to gain an edge in physical competition. If this analogy holds true, the use of such enhancers would be immoral.

Further, if the analogy holds, we already have a moral and legal framework in place for the time when mental enhancement is a reality – the rules for athletic competition can almost certainly be, with slight modifications, applied to academic competitions. It should come as no surprise if someday exam proctors ask for both photo IDs and urine samples.

Of course, mental competition is not limited to academics. It also takes place in the world of business. It is easy to imagine people using cognitive-enhancing drugs to gain an edge in the workplace against other employees they are competing with for raises, promotions and jobs. The companies themselves might encourage employees to use such products to gain a leg up on the competition.

An even fiercer arena of competition is the battle between nations. Once mental-enhancing products become available, it is certain that they will be pressed into service to serve the national interest of each country.

Unlike in academics and sports, there seems to be little concern about fair play in business and international competition. Thus, it can be expected that enhancement products will be used with little in the way of restraints or limits. Of course, given the nature of such competition, this might be morally acceptable. After all, it is not inherently immoral to use a better weapon than the enemy in order to defeat him.

An additional moral concern is the matter of side-effects. Physical enhancers, such as steroids, typically have negative side-effects and some of these can be quite serious. Despite these side-effects, many people have used them and have been harmed. It seems quite reasonable to believe that mental enhancers will have negative side-effects as well. If they are harmful, then using them would be morally questionable, at the very least. This is especially true in cases in which the user was pressured or forced to use them by their employer or government.

A final moral concern is the effect of such products on the person. While the nature of personal identity is a matter of great debate, it seems reasonable to believe that the mental attributes affected by such enhancers would play a role in personal identity. Thus, the use of such enhancers could conceivably alter the nature of the person. Hence, the use of such enhancers should not be taken lightly.

Memory and morality

In *The Matrix*, Trinity needs to fly a helicopter but does not know how. Fortunately, she simply downloads the requisite skill into her brain. This concept predates *The Matrix* and is a stock technology in Cyberpunk science fiction. The basic idea is that via a suitable technology, people can download skills and knowledge into their brains via implants that link to computer systems.

Like many technologies that began as science fiction, the capacity to download skills and information is on its way towards reality. Ed Berger,[57] a biomedical engineer at the University of Southern California, has developed chips and software that can (in theory) duplicate the function of brain cells. The basic idea is that the hardware chips act as replacements for the physical nerve cells and the software takes the place of the neural activity within the cells. In short, he is developing a technological analog to the organic brain.

While this technology is currently in a very early stage, it has great potential. Should the technology pan out, it could one day be used to treat people who have suffered damage to their brains, such as that brought about by Alzheimer's disease, strokes and head trauma. From a moral standpoint, these applications seem to be acceptable. After all, they would be on a par with existing treatments, such as medications, in that they merely aim at restoring capabilities that have been lost.

Not surprisingly, there are potential applications that do raise moral questions. In theory, the technology could be used to enable people to download skills and information without going through the current time-consuming and often tedious methods, such as attending classes.

While this application raises many moral concerns, four will be addressed here.

One concern is that since the technology is likely to be expensive, only wealthy people will be able to afford it for their own use, thus yielding an unfair advantage over the poor. The obvious response to this is that the rich already enjoy this advantage over the poor – they can already buy better education. This technology would simply allow them to purchase a better 'education' in a faster manner.

A second moral concern is that the need to stay competitive would drive people to undergo potentially risky surgery. In response, most technologies involve an element of danger and, of course, competitive people already put themselves in danger. For example, consider the automobile. It is likely that a competitive person will face an overall greater risk driving to and from work than they would face during surgery, even without factoring in the likelihood that they will be tired, distracted and talking on mobile phones while driving.

A third moral concern is that the technology will be used to cheat. One obvious example would be students downloading notes and texts to their memory chips and using this information to cheat on tests. In reply, it must be noted that the ability to cheat using information storage technology has existed since the invention of paper. The new technology would just enable cheaters to smuggle in more information and make it more difficult for teachers to catch them. As such, this aspect of the technology should not be considered any more immoral than paper and pen. It can also be argued that such technology would make testing people's ability to memorize obsolete. After all, one rationale behind testing this ability is that people need to rely on their memory because the information – for example, a book – will not always be readily available. However, with such technology this would no longer be the case and memory would no longer be an important attribute.

Another example is that people could cheat by downloading skills that they lack or have at a lower level of competence. For example, a student might download a writing program prior to writing a paper or a politician might download an enhancement to her rhetorical skills. While these uses would be morally questionable, the same effects are already being produced via different means. For example, students have long been turning in papers written by other people and politicians have relied on speechwriters since there have been politicians. Thus, the technology itself does not seem to be especially immoral – it would merely provide another means of doing what is already being done.

One final moral concern is that the technology could have the effect of impeding people's characters and mental abilities. Since people could easily acquire skills and information without effort, they would miss out on the character-building aspects of traditional education and learning (unless these can be downloaded as well . . .). The technology might also do to the mind what other technologies, such as automobiles, have done to the body. Just as many people have become overweight and physically unfit, perhaps such technology will result in people being mentally unfit.

It can be replied that just as some people still bike and run despite the existence of the automobile, it is likely that some people would still elect to exercise their brains the 'old fashioned way'. Thus, the technology would give people a choice – just as people can now choose between being physically unfit and physically fit. As such, the technology is no more morally questionable than the automobile. However, it must be noted that this concern is a reasonable one and is well worth considering as the technology progresses.

The case for nanoweapons

Advances in nanotechnology have made nanoweapons a very real possibility. Put briefly, a nanoweapon would consist of nanomachines and the intended use of the machines would be to inflict harm on an enemy. These nanomachines would be tiny robots that share a very important trait with living organisms: they would be capable of replication using resources gathered from the environment.

It might be wondered how such tiny machines could be used as effective weapons. As an answer, consider the army ant and bacteria. Army ants are rather small, yet can do terrible damage to whatever happens to have the misfortune of being caught in their path. Bacteria are even smaller than ants but, as the plague demonstrated very effectively, they can be extremely dangerous. Nanoweapons can take similar approaches. One type could function like army ants: simply disassembling their targets and using the raw materials to build more nanomachines which would, in turn, disassemble more targets and so on. Although it is rather gruesome to think about, human beings and other animals could serve quite nicely as 'food' for some types of nanomachines. Another type of nanoweapon could function like bacteria – entering the bodies of humans and other living things and doing, no doubt, terrible things.

Based on their programming, such nanoweapons could be targeted very specifically: a single building or perhaps even a single object (like a plane or missile) or person. They could, of course, also be much less discriminating. This, combined with their capacity for self-replication, gives nanoweapons the potential to be weapons of mass destruction.

Given the terrible potential of such weapons, it would seem reasonable to want to nip their development in the bud (assuming, of course, that they are not already being stockpiled). However, such weapons should be developed and a moral argument can be given in defence of this seemingly mad claim.

The ethical debates over nuclear weapons seem to have culminated, in general, in the view that the existence of such weapons of mass destruction is morally acceptable, provided that they serve to deter the very war they were created to fight. In any event, a strong case can be made that the weapons have, ironically, helped to keep the general peace – and this seems to be a good thing.

The deterrence value of nuclear weapons rests, in part, in their horrible nature – they are rightfully regarded as too horrible to use. Nanoweapons also seem to have this trait. A suitable nanoweapon could literally eat a city and its inhabitants alive – and this seems suitably horrifying. Thus, if nuclear weapons can be justified morally as deterrents, so too can certain nanoweapons.

It is, of course, reasonable to inquire as to why nanoweapons would be needed given the vast stockpiles of nuclear (not to mention biological and chemical) weapons that already exist. The answer is as follows.

Nuclear, chemical, biological and even conventional weapons have a major drawback – they only destroy. Nuclear weapons not only do vast amounts of damage, they also create massive radioactive contamination that can plague the earth for a very long time. Chemical and biological weapons, in addition to their initial harm, can also cause lasting damage to the environment and living creatures. Conventional weapons, like bombs, tend not to produce long-term effects but they can, of course, create a great deal of destruction.

It might be thought that nanoweapons would be as destructive as these other weapons, perhaps even worse. For example, one common concern among those who study nanotechnology is the problem of the 'grey goo'.[58] Put roughly, the problem is that self-replicating nanomachines could get out of hand and simply consume everything – leaving behind nothing but a 'grey goo' of nanomachines. Clearly, this could be far worse than the effects of any of the other weapons. Fortunately, nanoweapons could be programmed to limit their replication. Even more importantly, nanoweapons could be programmed to do more than replicate – they could also be programmed to build other things. For example, a nanoweapon could be designed that converts target structures and vehicles into raw materials suitable for future use. With suitable technological advances it would even be possible to develop nanoweapons that would literally turn, for example, tanks into tractors or military structures into houses. Thus, in addition to its quality as a weapon of terrible mass destruction nanoweapons, unlike the other weapons, could be designed to be far less 'destructive'. After all, if a city were hit with a nuclear weapon, all that would be left would be a radioactive nightmare. A city destroyed by a nanoweapon could be transformed into materials suitable for building another city.

As a final point, a massive war fought with nuclear, chemical and biological weapons would literally scorch the earth. A war fought with suitable nanoweapons might also result in the end of humanity – but the earth could survive nicely and be ready to give rise to a new species, hopefully one not so stupidly self-destructive.

RFID and privacy

Technological advances generally promise great things while also threatening to create problems. Radio Frequency Identification (RFID) is no exception to this general rule. An RFID system is similar in some ways to a bar code system in that it consists of a scanner that reads an information source. The main difference is that an RFID scanner scans information from tags containing circuits instead of from printed bars.

While there are many current and potential uses for RFID tags, the one that is currently generating the most controversy is the employment of RFID tags in tracking merchandise. On the face of it, this use of RFID tags seems perfectly harmless – they would be used to make inventory control more efficient. For example, as soon as tagged merchandise arrived in a store, an automatic system could detect the tags and log the information into the store database, all without a single box being opened. Despite the apparently benign nature of the tags, there has been some reluctance to use them.

This reluctance is fuelled in part by the fact that there are many moral concerns about the use of RFID tags. One concern is that the efficiency of the RFID systems will result in increased unemployment – fewer people will be needed to handle merchandise. While this is certainly a serious matter, it is not a problem specific to RFID systems. After all, people have been losing jobs to technology since there have been jobs.

A second concern and one fairly specific to RFID systems is that, in addition to tracking merchandise, RFID tags can be used to gather information about customers and even track them.

If a customer buys an item with a credit or debit card, then the item will be linked with that card (and, in most cases, to the purchaser). While companies will no doubt claim that this information will enable them to serve the customer better, privacy advocates are rather worried about the potential for abuse – simply imagine the increase in email spam and telemarketing once companies know exactly what you buy.

Of even greater concern is the fact that such purchases will create a 'data trail'. While such data trails exist today, RFID tags create the potential for a marked increase in the amount of data available. For example, if a couple were going through a divorce, the wife could learn, perhaps via a private detective accessing RFID data, that the unfaithful husband's recent 'naughty' lingerie purchase took place when he claimed to be at work and that, while it is not in her size, it would nicely fit that person he is 'just friends' with.

What is perhaps of the greatest concern to privacy advocates is the fact that the RFID tags in our possessions (such as mobile phones) could enable other people to track us – perhaps not quite as dramatically as in movies like *Enemy of the State* or *Minority Report* but with a reasonable degree of effectiveness nonetheless. This would enable organizations, such as governments, and even individuals to learn, through the use of suitably powerful RFID readers, where and when a person has been. For example, the detective hired by the above-mentioned wife might acquire RFID data showing that the husband and his 'friend' were in the same hotel room at the same time while he was allegedly at the dentist's.

One reasonable reply to the concerns about data trails and tracking is that only people who are committing misdeeds (such as having affairs, breaking the law or plotting terrorism) have anything to worry about. Do we, it should be asked, have a moral right to conceal our misdeeds? It would seem rather odd, perhaps even a contradiction, to claim a moral right to conceal one's wrongdoings.

An equally reasonable response to this reply is that even people who are not doing misdeeds still have a right to worry. Simply considering the track record of governments, even democratic ones such as in the United States and the United Kingdom, would give any citizen grounds for concerns. For example, one has but to do a little research into the Patriot Act's application in America to realize that there are very serious grounds for concern. And, of course, there are equally serious concerns that companies and individuals would misuse such information to the detriment of others. After all, as the Iron Law of Technological Misuse states: any technology that can be misused will be misused.[59]

One last worry is that one can easily imagine enterprising criminals using RFID readers to scan potential victims, luggage or buildings for things worth stealing.

Given these concerns, the implementation of any such RFID systems is a matter that should be given serious thought.

Gene therapy and sports

The use of enhancements to cheat in sports is nothing new. However, advances in gene therapy have opened the door to a new type of cheating: genetic enhancement. Not surprisingly, these advances raise various moral issues and some of these will be discussed below.

Gene therapy was originally intended to help patients suffering from the effects of disease or old age. For example, extensive research has been conducted on the use of gene therapy to spur on new muscle growth in people suffering from muscular dystrophy.[60] Such medical applications are quite laudable.

However, as countless examples have shown, any technology that can be misused will be misused. The misuse of gene therapy is most likely to involve the enhancement of athletes. While there are many possibilities, some likely approaches involve using therapy to promote rapid increase in muscle mass (for increased strength) or to enhance the number of red blood cells (for increased endurance). Such applications seem somewhat less than laudable.

At first glance, using gene therapy to gain a competitive edge seems as immoral as using performance-enhancing drugs, such as steroids. After all, using either would be cheating – the acquisition of an unearned, unfair advantage. The advantage would be unearned because it does not stem from the athlete's own relevant abilities and efforts. The advantage would be unfair because it is not something that would be available to everyone.

Interestingly, if cheating is defined this way, then many accepted practices in athletics are actually ways of cheating. Two examples are as follows. First, there is the use of special (and expensive) gear such as custom racing bikes and highly advanced swim suits. Given that most athletes do not make or design such items themselves, it should be concluded that these items yield an unfair, unearned advantage. For example, if Bill beats Sam because Bill's sponsor can afford to equip Bill with the latest and greatest racing bike, then Bill has cheated just as much as if he had used a performance-enhancing drug or gene therapy. After all, in both cases Bill's win rests on an external factor and not solely on his abilities or efforts.

Second, some athletes receive professional training and coaching which can involve the use of multimillion dollar facilities, computer-enhanced training, personal medical care, and other such services. Given that the athletes are being coached, trained and serviced like high-performance machines rather than simply relying on their own abilities and efforts, they are gaining an unfair, unearned advantage. For example, if Sally beats Jane in road races because Sally can afford a personal trainer, visits to running clinics and so on, then she has cheated just as much as if she had used gene therapy or a performance-enhancing drug. This is because her victory depended on the purchased efforts of others, rather than on her abilities and efforts.

It might be objected that the advantages described above are not cheating because they can be earned – Bill's efforts as a biker got him the sponsorship and Sally's success in business gave her the money to spend on trainers. Of course, the same reasoning could be applied to gene therapy or performance-enhancing drugs – a person could earn the money to buy them.

It could be objected that the advantages described above are fair because they are available to everyone. The obvious answer is that this simply is not the case. Another answer is that enhancing drugs and gene therapy would be just as available, if not more so.

Finally, it might be objected that there is a morally relevant difference between the use of gene therapy and the advantages described above. While there are differences between the methods, most of these differences do not seem to be morally relevant. This is because all of them yield advantages that do not stem from the relevant efforts or abilities of the athletes.

One point worth considering is that the medical enhancements seem to be more effective than the other methods. However, this does not affect their moral status – using a more effective means of stealing does not make less effective methods of stealing any less wrong.

Thus, it would seem that gene therapy should not be considered cheating unless, of course, the above-mentioned methods are also considered cheating. In fact, it could be argued that gene therapy is not only not cheating but a way to level the playing field.

Research has shown that there is truth behind the old joke that the way to be a world-class athlete is to train hard and pick your parents wisely. While training is obviously important, it has been found that people with the 'right' genes have a significant advantage over others. It is obvious that people do not earn their genes and, as such, it could be argued that people with certain genes have an unfair advantage. While nothing could be done about this in the past, gene therapy provides a means of eliminating this unearned advantage: all athletes could be made genetically 'equal', thus making the competition fairer.

Gender selection

Parents have often desired to have a child of a particular gender. In the past, various 'folk' methods have been used to set gender before birth, but these proved to be rather ineffective. However, medical science has provided two methods of gender selection.[61] The first method, which includes the fairly simple Ericsson method and the more complex MicroSort method, involve separating sperm with X chromosomes (girl-producing) from sperm containing Y chromosomes (boy-producing). The appropriate sperm is then used to impregnate the woman. While the sorting methods increase the odds of getting the desired gender, there is still a significant chance of getting the other gender.

For those who would prefer better odds (and who have the necessary funds) there is a third option known as preimplanation genetic diagnosis. In this method, eggs are removed from the woman and fertilized in a Petri dish. These embryos are allowed to grow and are then genetically tested for X (girl) and Y (boy) chromosomes. The desired embryos are then implanted and, if all goes well, the end result will be the boy or girl the parents want.

Not surprisingly, the use of gender selection creates a variety of ethical problems.

First, there is the general question of whether it is right for people to make such a choice. Assuming that it is morally acceptable for people to make the initial decision to have a child, it would seem to follow that choosing the gender would also be acceptable. After all, the decision to have a child seems to be a morally greater decision than the decision to select the gender. Also, consider the following analogy: if a person has a right to decide whether to buy a car or not, she would certainly seem to have the right to pick the model. It would be odd, to say the least, for dealers to insist that although you can decide whether to buy a car, you must spin a wheel to determine the model. Thus, gender selection does seem acceptable.

It might be contended that gender selection is 'unnatural' or that it 'crosses a line'. However, it does not seem any more unnatural than using antibiotics, flying in aircraft, or using ultrasound. Also, it does not seem to 'cross a line' that has not already been crossed by the use of birth control or abstinence – means that allow people to choose whether to even have a child or not.

It might also be contended that it is against God's will. However, given that God is all-powerful and all-knowing, if he did not want it to happen, then he would simply prevent it from happening.

Second, there is the moral concern that parents will be morally accountable to the child for choosing his or her gender. For example, if the parents chose a boy but he eventually realizes that he really wants to be a mother, the parents would have wronged him and he might blame them for this. A possible reply is that it seems likely that some children will blame their parents for not using such a selection, thus leaving their gender up to chance. Another reply is that the moral accountability created by deciding the gender of the child is dwarfed by the moral accountability generated by deciding to have a child at all. A final reply is that there is something rather suspicious about the view that leaving something up to chance rather than making a conscious choice somehow gets a person off the moral hook. For example, this reasoning would seem to entail that if the child was planned, then the parents would be accountable, but if the child resulted from an accident (such as a broken condom), the parents would not be accountable.

Third, there is the concern that the use of such methods will create a gender gap – it is generally assumed that parents will select more boys than girls. In support of this assumption, people often point to the parts of Asia where the practices of aborting female foetuses and killing female babies are still considered acceptable. While this is a legitimate concern, it must be noted that, in the United States, parents using these methods have selected roughly equal numbers of boys and girls. Further, it is unlikely that such methods, which can be very expensive and complex, will be used widely enough to impact the human population in any significant way. Further, even if it does become widespread in, for example, the above-mentioned parts of Asia, gender selection of this type seems morally preferable to abortions and infanticide.

Thus, even though there are reasonable concerns regarding gender selection, it would seem to be morally acceptable.

Ownership and wayward genes

The genetic modification of food crops has generated a great deal of controversy and concern. One court case in this area has raised an interesting ethical issue. Monsanto, the owner of Roundup Ready seed, accused a Canadian farmer, Percy Schmeiser, of planting its modified canola seed on his farm without purchasing a licence from the company.[62] Schmeiser countered this charge by asserting that the seed he planted, which belonged to him, had been contaminated by his neighbour's fields or by spilled seed. Hence, there was no legitimate reason for him to pay a licensing fee – the seed he planted was his and it was not his fault that it had been genetically contaminated. Not surprisingly, the judge ruled in favour of Monsanto – how the seed ended up in the fields did not matter. What was important was that Monsanto owned the rights to the modified seed and Schmeiser had not licensed its use from the company.

At first glance, it might seem that the judge simply enforced reasonable property rights. In defence of this, consider the following analogy. Suppose Sue writes a book and copyrights the text. Copies of the book are purchased by Sam's bookstore and a copy, quite by accident, ends up in a nearby bookstore owned by Jack. Finding the book, Jack scans it into a computer and prints copies of his own to sell from his bookstore. When arrested, he tells the judge that the book found its way into his store by accident. In this case it seems quite clear that Jack is in the wrong. He has no moral or legal right to sell the copies he has made, even if the first copy ended up in his store by accident.

While this analogy is appealing, there is a serious problem that makes the analogy fail. The problem is that plants exchange genetic information – this is called gene flow. This gene flow involves genetic information spreading from engineered crops to other plants – most typically closely related plants. For example, if a field of modified wheat is planted near a field of unmodified wheat, it is quite likely that future generations of the previously unmodified wheat will be found to contain the modified genes. After all, pollen-transferring insects, seed-transferring wildlife and the wind generally fail to respect property rights. That such contamination occurs is shown by a study noted by the May 2002 *National Geographic* magazine.[63] In this study 20 products sold as being 'modification free' were examined. Fifty-five per cent of them were found to be contaminated with modified ingredients and 25 per cent were significantly contaminated. This contamination was accidental and took place despite efforts to use crops that were not modified.

Given this bit of information, another analogy should help clear up the ethics of the situation a little. Suppose that MikeSoft has developed a word processing program, MikeSoft Word. MikeSoft dutifully takes all the needed legal steps to confirm and protect the ownership of the software code. Now, suppose that MikeSoft Word works very well but that parts of its code get distributed via the internet whenever a user is connected. This code integrates itself, virus-like, into other word processing programs. It does no damage and, in fact, often adds new and desirable features to the other software. Imagine that a competitor attempts to sell a program called WordAlmostPerfect that has been accidentally contaminated with the code from MikeSoft Word. Learning of this, the CEO of MikeSoft is outraged and slaps the company that made WordAlmostPerfect with a lawsuit for using the code in its product.

MikeSoft does, of course, own the code in question and it would be unethical for another party simply to steal it from the company. This right is recognized by the law in most countries. However, it is ethically irresponsible for MikeSoft to allow its code to contaminate other programs and it would be ludicrous for the company to claim ownership of the software it had infected. To do so would be like one landowner claiming he owns his neighbour's lot as well as his own because his dog answered nature's call on her lot. In such a case it is obvious that he does not own her lot and is, in fact, obligated to keep his 'property' off her lawn.

Thus, while ownership rights do protect the right to the property in question, it would also seem that they obligate the owner to make sure that his/her property does not contaminate the property of others. Unless such protection can be assured, companies that sell modified seeds have no moral grounds for demanding that farmers license their seeds (except in cases where they can show that the farmer actually stole the seed).

Is biomimicry bad?

Biomimicry, a term made popular by Janine Benyus, refers to the field of finding solutions to problems by mimicking aspects of nature. Some types of biomimicry are entirely uncontroversial. For example, the very useful invention Velcro was inspired by burrs sticking to a dog. Other types of biomimicry raise serious moral questions. For example, scientists who work for Nexia[64] have genetically modified goats so that they will produce spider silk in their milk. The company hopes to be able to gather the liquid silk and then, with the technological help of the US Army, weave the silk into threads for a variety of applications. Other types of biomimicry involve similar types of genetic modifications and it is these cases that raise the most serious moral concerns.

The products of such biomimicry have the potential to do a great deal of good. For example, it is hoped that the artificial spider silk threads could be used in a process by which replacement human ligaments could be grown. It can, of course, be argued that such potential benefits (not to mention the potential profits) provide a moral (or at least a monetary) justification for such genetic modifications. After all, the argument might go, who could be opposed to something that could help injured people?

Despite the potential benefits, such modifications do raise serious moral concerns. One concern is both moral and pragmatic: such modifications might pose a danger. While it is rather unlikely that any science-fiction-style monsters will be spawned by such experiments and run amok, such genetic modifications could create organisms that pose risks to humans. For example, natural bacteria are bad enough and modified bacteria could be a very serious medical risk. Because of such potential dangers, it might be wise to heed the advice of Harvard biologist Ruth Hubbard[65] and proceed very carefully in such matters. After all, aside from the financially based desire to register patents first, there seems to be no compelling need to rush in such matters when so much is at stake.

A second concern is that it might be wrong to exploit organisms by transforming them into living factories. It can be countered that humans already use animals as living factories (harvesting their milk and eggs, for example) and that animals have been modified by selective breeding for centuries. Thus, those who have made use of this sort of biomimicry have done nothing worse than the farmers who selectively bred cows to produce more milk. Some, like philosopher Peter Singer, might reply to this by arguing that such exploitation is morally wrong whether it involves biomimicry or not. Such arguments are typically made on utilitarian grounds: the suffering of the animals morally outweighs the benefits that humans receive from exploiting them. Thus, those who have made use of this sort of biomimicry have done something just as bad as the farmers who selectively bred cows to produce more milk.

While the morality of the general exploitation of animals cannot be settled here, it does seem that biomimicry involving genetic modifications involves a moral step beyond existing practices of animal exploitation. It is one thing, perhaps a bad thing, to exploit goats for their milk and meat. It is quite another to alter their fundamental nature so that they produce spider silk. While the 'natural law' of 'tooth and claw' might justify eating goats or milking them (the law of 'stool and bucket'?), it does seem difficult to justify modifying them.

A third and final concern focuses more on humanity than on the potential targets of modification. While it is clear that organisms subjected to such modifications will be changed, it also seems likely that humanity will be altered as well. By this I do not mean that humans will modify themselves (but that fate, no doubt, awaits us like a mugger in the dark alley of the future). Rather, I mean that by coming to regard living creatures not only as commodities but also as commodities to be altered freely to suit our whims, we will have lost yet another fragment of our humanity. And, of course, these days we have so little to spare.

8   Medical Ethics

The Hippocratic Oath shows the strong connection between medicine and ethics. This subsection looks at the morality of using lies to heal as well as denying people tasty, yet possibly deadly, food in the interest of their health.

Fat, bacteria and the state

During the later months of 2006, food problems made the news in the United States. One type of problem involved contaminated food. Although the United States has fairly strict regulations regarding meat, the government provides little regulation in regards to produce. This lack of proper regulation no doubt played a role in allowing produce contaminated with e-coli to reach supermarkets and fast food restaurants and thus make people sick. Not surprisingly, these e-coli outbreaks prompted calls for stricter government regulations.

A second problem involved trans fat. In December 2006, New York City banned trans fat in its restaurants and this inspired others to consider imposing their own bans. Bans on trans fat would result in extensive changes since trans fats are either ingredients in or used in the preparation of a wide variety of foods. Not surprisingly, the food served at most fast food restaurants tends to be laden with trans fats.

While most agree that trans fat makes foods taste better, it is supposed to contribute to heart disease and increase 'bad' cholesterol while decreasing 'good' cholesterol. It is the health threat posed by trans fat that is used to justify the ban.

While the cases of e-coli contamination and the trans fat bans might not seem closely related, they raise an important moral issue about the limits of governmental protection (or interference). It is to this matter that I now turn.

It is generally accepted that the modern state has the moral right to protect its citizens from harms. Further, many thinkers contend that the state has a moral obligation to provide such protection. While there is a general consensus about the overall role of the state, there is extensive disagreement when it comes to the details.

In regards to determining when government protection would be morally acceptable, three main factors are the nature of the harm, whether or not such protection would violate any freedoms or rights, and whether or not such protection would be regarded as undesirable by the people.

In the case of e-coli contamination, the matter seems rather clear-cut. Contaminated food presents a clear danger to the health of the citizens. Intuitively, one would be hard pressed to argue that growers and distributors should be allowed the freedom to provide contaminated foods to the public. This would be on a par with arguing that people should have the right randomly to attack each other and that hardly seems like a right that should be granted. Naturally, it would be rather shocking for any sane individual to express a desire to eat contaminated foods. Quite the contrary, people strongly desire to avoid contaminated foods. Given the plausibility of these three claims, government action to protect people from e-coli contaminated food is morally acceptable.

In contrast with the e-coli case, the trans fat case provides significant room for debate. As was the case with e-coli contamination, the discussion will focus on the three factors presented above.

In regards to harm, the evidence points towards trans fats being somewhat harmful. As mentioned above, trans fat is linked to heart disease and can have an undesirable effect on cholesterol levels. The fact that it is harmful provides the most compelling moral argument for the ban. After all, if the state should protect people from food contaminated with e-coli, then it would seem that it should also protect them from food contaminated with trans fat.

In regards to the desirability of the protection offered by the ban, the news stories indicate that opinions are rather mixed. Those who support the ban tend to find the health argument compelling. Those who oppose the ban tend to do so either because they rather like the flavour added by trans fat or because they believe that people should be free to decide what they eat. This leads to the second main factor in this case, namely that of freedom.

A morally compelling argument against the ban can be based on freedom. Being a competent adult gives a person the freedom or right to make informed life choices. Many of these choices involve risks. For example, going on a hike in the woods puts a person at risk – falling, getting lost or being trapped by bad weather are all possibilities. As another example, driving to the store puts a person at risk – an automobile accident is always a possibility (over 40,000 people a year are killed in automobile accidents in the United States alone).[66] As a final example, almost all sports put a person at risk of injuries. Despite the potential for harm, it seems most reasonable for adults to use their own judgement in such cases. The same would apply to the case of trans fat – it should be left to the individual to decide.

This position can be further justified as follows. The main justification for banning trans fat is that it is harmful to physical health. While physical health is a good, it is not the only good. Freedom of choice certainly seems to be a good on a par with that of physical health. While a ban on trans fat would protect people from a health harm, it would do so by harming their freedom of choice. Taking a utilitarian approach, the harm done to freedom would seem to exceed the rather minor health advantages to be gained from banning trans fat. Thus, the ban does not seem to be morally justifiable and the choice should remain with the individual.

It might be objected that people often eat trans fat in ignorance – not knowing that it is harmful or not knowing that it is in their food. This is a reasonable concern – a person cannot make an informed choice without being informed. Given that trans fats are potentially harmful, it would be reasonable to require that restaurants and manufacturers make that information readily available to the consumer – much like alcohol and tobacco products come with warnings. As long as the decision is an informed one, then people should retain the right to choose trans fat – just as they can now choose tobacco, alcohol and automobiles (all of which are far more dangerous than trans fat).

Lies . . . the best medicine?

In July 2002 a study was published by the *New England Journal of Medicine* on the subject of arthroscopic surgery.[67] In addition to addressing medical issues, the study also raises an ethical issue in regards to the use of placebos.

In brief, the study focused on arthroscopic knee surgery and involved two main groups of patients: one received real surgery and the other underwent 'fake' surgery which simulated the actual surgery. The patients who underwent the 'fake' surgery claimed they felt better after the process and, interestingly enough, were able to walk and climb stairs faster than those who had undergone the real surgery. The benefits of the 'surgery' were, of course, purely psychological: the patients believed they were better, so they felt better.

While the placebo effect does seem to benefit patients, there is still the issue of whether or not it is ethical for doctors to use it in the treatment of patients.

On one side of the issue is the view that such treatment is unethical. The case for this is as follows. By definition, the use of placebos in treatment involves deceiving the patient – the effect arises because the patient believes in the efficacy of the alleged treatment. If the doctor was honest and convinced the patient that the treatment was a mere deception, the treatment would, of course, not be effective. Given that it is, in general, wrong to deceive people, it would then follow that such deception in medicine would be wrong. If the fact is taken into account that the doctor is a professional who is expected to be honest in her dealings with patients, such deception seems all the more onerous. Thus, such deceptive treatments should not be used.

On the other side of the issue is the view that while lying is generally not good, a deception in such situations is acceptable. The case for this is as follows. First, there are cases in which beneficial deception is acceptable. For example, children are told about Santa Claus, the Easter Bunny and the Tooth Fairy because it brings extra happiness into their lives. As another example, people are sometimes told lies to avoid causing them suffering or to spare their feelings. If such lying is justified (which it seems to be), then the use of the placebo effect to ease patients' pain and aid their recovery seems perfectly acceptable and perhaps even commendable.

Second, while philosophers and scientists are under a professional moral obligation to be truthful, medical doctors are not under this same obligation. The proper goal of philosophy and science is truth and thus those who enter these professions are obligated to the truth. The proper goal of medicine is not truth. The proper goal of medicine is the relieving of pain and the curing of ills. It seems reasonable that doctors should be allowed to use various means to achieve this proper end of their discipline. If deception, in the form of placebos, can help achieve this goal, then their use is no more unethical than the use of surgery or medication. Thus, since placebos are just one more means of treatment, their use is morally acceptable.

Finally, the placebo effect works without the use of surgery or actual medications. Given the potentially dangerous side-effects of even fairly innocuous drugs and the hazards of even minor surgery, it would seem that the use of effective placebos is morally acceptable. After all, such treatment brings about the desired effect with less risk.

It might be objected that even though the patients might feel better, nothing has really been done for them. On one hand, this is a reasonable concern. It would be unforgivable for doctors simply to cover up illnesses and injuries with placebos instead of actually treating them for real. On the other hand, there are many cases in which the main problem is pain. While being injured or ill is an objective matter (a person is or is not hurt or ill regardless of what she thinks about her condition), pain is subjective. Being in pain is simply feeling pain. So, if a person does not feel the pain, they are not in pain. In such cases the placebo effect would seem to be a reasonable and morally acceptable treatment.

9 Media and Ethics

The media culture is rife with moral matters . . . or, more aptly put, immoral matters. Lies, murder, secrets and more: all the ingredients for a hit show or a philosophical provocation.

A million (not so) little lies

The entire world, or at least the popular media, was recently shocked by the revelation that bestselling author James Frey had fabricated or exaggerated significant portions of his book *A Million Little Pieces*.[68] While yet another insignificant scandal of this nature might seem to lack philosophical merit, the situation does actually raise some important and meaningful ethical issues about honesty and lies.

While most moral philosophers have regarded lying as wrong, there have been some notable exceptions. Plato, for example, allowed for what he called the 'noble lie'. Plato, normally rather scrupulous about truth, justified the lie in terms of the benefits it had for the ideal society he envisioned in the *Republic*.[69] Other thinkers have justified lying on similar grounds – a lie, it can be argued, is morally acceptable provided that the positive consequences of the lie outweigh the negative consequences. The classic example, used in countless philosophy classes, involves lying to a killer in order to save a person's life. Since the judgement about lying in such cases is intuitively appealing, it follows that lying can be morally acceptable in certain circumstances.

Oprah Winfrey, who shapes (or provides) the opinions of millions of people, phoned in just such a consequentialist defence of Frey on the Larry King show. After it had been revealed that Frey was somewhat less than honest in his book, Oprah asserted that 'the underlying message of redemption in James Frey's memoir still resonates with me'. While she did not present an explicit argument in his defence, her view seems to have been that the overall message matters more than the truth of the claims within the work. In short, the lies are acceptable provided that the consequences are good. Of course, it must be noted that Oprah later changed her view of Mr Frey and called him to task for his deception.[70]

Oprah's initial position has a certain appeal to it. If a work can influence people in a positive way, then the question of whether it is fiction or not seems somehow secondary. What matters, it might be claimed, is the effect of the work. To use an analogy – if my lie saves the life of an innocent person, then what is morally significant is the saving of that life. Although I lied, that is not what is important. In the case of Frey's book it could be argued that if some people are inspired to seek their own redemption, then their redemption is what is of moral concern – not the accuracy of the story that helped them in that direction.

Naturally, some people were very critical of Frey as soon as his fabrications were revealed. Mary Karr, ironically the author of her own memoir entitled *The Liar's Club*, said that 'manufacturing events wholesale is just morally wrong. I think it calls into question every aspect of this guy – who he is and everything in his damn book.'[71]

Karr's stated position is certainly plausible. One way to defend her view is to use an argument based on the consequences of the lies. As she notes, the fact that Frey lied in his work does undermine his credibility. Given that he admits to making up and exaggerating many events in his book, there are good grounds to be sceptical about the rest of the book and Mr Frey himself. This scepticism can have negative consequences for his message of redemption. The fact that the work contains lies would certainly seem to undermine its power to inspire and might actually show that Mr Frey is not so redeemed after all.

It might be countered, as was argued above, that what matters is the message of the book and that the truth or falsity of the claims is secondary. A somewhat obvious reply to this counter is that a category already exists for works that involve made-up events: fiction. Hence, there would seem to be no reason to lie and call the book non-fiction in order to get the message across. An inspirational work containing made-up events can be published as fiction and still produce the inspirational effects – but without the lies.

To be fair to Frey, he did initially try to sell his book as a piece of fiction. But, as fiction, it was rejected more than a dozen times. When, at his agent's suggestion, he relabelled it as a non-fiction memoir he was able to sell it to a publisher . . . who then was able to sell millions of copies. This does raise a final argument in favour of lying. If labelling a work as a memoir enables it to reach and possibly inspire millions of people, then the lies could be justified (once again) on the grounds of the consequences. If the work had remained a novel, it might have never seen print. By lying, Frey's work became a success and has perhaps helped inspire some people on their own road to redemption. Then again, it also might have inspired more people to become liars or even disillusioned them as to the possibilities of redemption.

Anonymous ethics

For the press and the people, anonymous sources within democratic governments have long been an important source of information. The most famous example is, of course, Deep Throat in the American Watergate case.

On the face of it, it seems morally acceptable for an anonymous source to reveal governmental misdeeds. Intuitively, the citizens of a democratic government have a right to know what is occurring within their government and anonymous sources play an important role in providing the people, via the press, with such information. Of course, not everyone regards anonymous sources as acceptable and there are various moral concerns about such sources.

One concern is that by choosing to remain anonymous a person is being a moral coward who is willing to make claims and perhaps even accusations but is not willing to accept responsibility for his or her actions. In the case of accusations, it seems reasonable to expect that the accuser makes him- or herself known. Accusations from the shadows, one might argue, are just a bit too sinister for democracies. Thus it seems that there are good grounds for considering anonymous sources to be immoral.

The worry about accusations from the shadows is a reasonable concern. Of course, the fact that democracies need people in the shadows to expose the various misdeeds that occur in those same shadows is far more sinister.

In reply to the charge of moral cowardice, an analogy can be drawn between anonymous sources and undercover agents. For an agent to make her true identity known would not be an act of moral courage. Rather, it would be an act of stupidity – she would no longer be able to perform her job and would probably be harmed. The same is true of anonymous sources. In order to continue to provide information to the press, an anonymous source must remain anonymous. It is likely that in many cases the good done by passing on such information can outweigh the charge of moral cowardice. Further, avoiding the harm that is likely to be inflicted in spiteful retaliation does not seem like moral cowardice – it seems like good sense.

It might be further objected that anonymous sources are just that – agents, or more bluntly, spies for the press within the government. Like any spies, they should be exposed and neutralized before they can reveal any more secrets and thus do more harm.

In response, a spy is typically regarded as doing wrong because they are stealing information and conveying it to the enemies of the nation. An anonymous source that is revealing information to the press of that country does not seem to be stealing. After all, the press is conveying that information to the people and the people are the ones who own the government. One cannot steal what one has a right to – so there is no theft. Further, the press is conveying the information primarily to the people and not to an enemy. Or so one would hope – if the people and their government are enemies then there is much more to worry about than anonymous sources.

It might be countered that although the source is revealing it to the press, enemies of the nation also gain access to this information. So, the source is indirectly acting as a spy for enemies of the state. While this concern is sensible – revealing damaging information (like technical information or military plans) would be of great moral concern – most cases do not involve the revelation of secrets that would be of use to an enemy. Also, it is likely that foreign powers know a lot more about what is going on than the citizens do. One might even suspect that governments are more in the business of keeping secrets from their own citizens than from each other.

One final concern is the matter of loyalty. Members of the government, it can be argued, should be loyal to the government and not reveal their doings to the press without due authorization. This concern is quite reasonable because loyalty is a virtue and an organization cannot function well without trust. However, a democratic government is supposed to derive its authority from the people and is supposed to exist for the good of the people. While governments typically exist for the good of those in power and their fellows, there is a clear distinction between the reality of the situation and the morality of the situation. As such, while those in power do expect loyalty from their fellows at the expense of the good of the people, they have no moral right to expect that loyalty. Instead, the loyalty of the members of the government should be given to the people. Thus, when a member of the government is aware of misdeeds within the government, they have the right and perhaps even an obligation to report these misdeeds to the press so that the people will know what their government is doing.

Anonymous sources

While anonymous sources have been utilized for quite some time by journalists, recent years have seen a rather substantial increase in their use. While journalism is often seen as being quite distinct from philosophy, this increasing use of anonymous sources raises interesting philosophical problems.

The first problem is a straightforward matter in the realm of critical thinking. When a journalist (or anyone) cites a source to support a claim, they are using an argument from authority. The basic idea is that the claim should be accepted as true because the person cited is a legitimate expert in the field and is therefore likely to say true things in her field. The quality of the argument rests, naturally enough, on the quality of the alleged expert. The quality of an expert is assessed in terms of a variety of factors, such as the person's education, degree of bias, positions held and amount of experience. If the expert in question is a legitimate expert, then the claims she makes in her field should be regarded as very plausible and typically accepted as true.

One obvious problem with anonymous sources is that the audience has little, if any, basis upon which to assess the quality of the alleged authority. At most the audience might be given vague information about the person's job. For example, the source might be identified as 'a high government official' or 'a military expert on terrorism'. Given such a dearth of information, the audience cannot make a reasonable judgement about the quality of the source and hence cannot reasonably accept the claim as plausible on the basis of the alleged authority.

Of course, journalists do expect the audience to believe these claims. If they did not, they would obviously not bother to report them. Since the authorities are not adequately identified, another basis is needed for the audience to accept such claims rationally. In such cases, the audience is supposed to accept that the claims made by the source are correct because the journalist accepts them as a legitimate expert. In short, the audience is relying on the critical thinking ability of the journalist. Unfortunately for the audience, journalists are generally not experts in critical thinking nor do they tend to be experts in the areas they are writing about. Because of this lack of expertise, there are reasonable grounds for concern when journalists rely on anonymous sources. To be specific, unless it has been established that the journalist is adequately skilled at assessing the expertise of her sources, then there is no reason to accept the anonymous sources as credible on the basis of the journalist's say-so. This is not to say that the claims should be rejected, but the rational course is to suspend judgement in regards to such claims.

Despite this serious problem, there are good reasons to maintain the anonymity of a source. One reason to keep a source anonymous is so that the source can continue to provide information. This is analogous to the situation of a spy: a spy must remain unknown in order to keep sending information. In cases in which exposure would put an end to the source, then preserving the anonymity of the source would be justified on the practical ground that anonymous information is better than no information.

Another reason for a source to remain anonymous is that the source could be harmed if her identity became known. In some cases, this concern is quite reasonable and justifies the decision to keep the source anonymous. For example, if a person is exposing the activities of a criminal organization or terrorists to the press, then she has a good and acceptable reason to remain anonymous – namely that of staying alive.

What is rather worrisome is the fact that many anonymous sources are within supposedly democratic governments. In many cases the journalists make it evident that their sources choose to remain anonymous out of fear of retaliation for speaking to the press. While there are no doubt cases in which sources should not be talking to the press, there are still serious moral concerns here.

The fact that many sources choose to remain anonymous out of fear indicates that at least some people in power will punish those who are willing to inform the public about what is happening in their own government. In some cases such punishment would be morally acceptable. For example, such punishment would be acceptable if a source was acting out of malice or revealing secrets that would be harmful to the general good. In other cases, such punishment would be morally unacceptable. For example, such punishment would be wrong if the source revealed the misdeeds of officials or information about potential harm to the general good. Those who would be punished for doing what is right naturally bring to mind the fate of Socrates – he revealed the truth about those in power and paid for this with his life. As Socrates argued, those in power should be grateful for having such gadflies to keep them on the path they are supposed to be

walking. But, as Socrates found, the unjust tend to prefer to stick to
their misdeeds and remain in the shadows. Since it is unreasonable to
expect everyone to have the courage of Socrates, it seems acceptable
to preserve the anonymity of such sources in order to protect them
from harm while affording them the opportunity to expose misdeeds
in government. Of course, the ideal would be to eliminate the need for
anonymous sources by ensuring that those in power are not unjust,
vindictive or needlessly secretive. Given that this is very unlikely,
anonymous sources seem to be here to stay and justifiably so in some
cases.

Murder, money and the media

Each time that it seems that the media cannot sink any lower, another
event comes along to show that they can, in fact, plumb new depths.
One deep dive involves the News Corporation and O. J. Simpson.
Two companies owned by this corporation, ReganBooks and Fox,
considered presenting 'O. J. Simpson: If I Did It, Here's How It
Happened' in a book and a television show. It was eventually decided
that this was a bad idea and the book and show were cancelled.[72] In
the book and show Simpson tells how he would have committed the
murders he has long insisted he did not commit. Not surprisingly,
this situation raises a variety of moral issues.

One moral issue is whether or not the media should present such
things to the world.

One moral reason why they should not is that by doing so they are
rewarding people for evil actions. In the case of O. J., he is being well
paid for describing either a terrible crime he did commit or how he
would have committed such a terrible crime. While the first situation
is far worse, the second situation is still morally questionable.

When people commit evil actions, our intuitions tell us that the
morally correct response is to punish them. This punishment is generally justified in terms of rehabilitation, retribution or deterrence.
Rehabilitation aims at leading the person away from evil. Retribution

is generally seen as balancing the books and paying back the miscreant for the misdeed. For example, a thief might be forced to make restitutions for what she stole. Deterrence is, of course, intended to decrease the chances of the misdeed being perpetrated again. Rewarding those who do evil by giving them book deals and TV shows runs directly counter to these moral intuitions. Rewarding them in this manner hardly serves to rehabilitate or deter them: rewarding a type of behaviour is the way to get a person to continue that behaviour – and perhaps to encourage others to behave that way as well. Rewarding them in this way is hardly retribution. In fact, it is the exact opposite of retribution – the person is rewarded for evil. Thus, such action by media companies is wrong.

It might be objected that the media is not rewarding the person for his misdeeds, but simply buying the story. However, paying a person with money or fame for their evil deeds certainly seems to be rewarding them.

A second reason is that by providing such rewards the media might motivate others to commit similar evil deeds. While it is difficult to establish what influence such shows and books might have on people, it seems reasonable to think that they do have some influence. Given that people are motivated to seek fame and fortune, it is not unreasonable to think that people will commit crimes or claim they committed crimes in order to be rewarded by the media. One recent example of this is the case of John Mark Karr. By falsely claiming to have murdered JonBenet Ramsey, he was rewarded with international fame (or infamy) and an appearance on the Larry King Live show on CNN.

It might be objected that the media influence is relatively weak and that it affects very few people. After all, it can be argued, few people will be inclined to kill their spouses or lie about killing a child just to be on television. For those with utilitarian leanings, it can also be argued that the entertainment value provided by watching such shows and reading such books outweighs the harm caused by those influenced by the media.

It can be replied that even if the influence is weak, the media is still morally culpable as a contributing factor and that entertainment value does not justify creating such harms. Of course, their responsibility would only be proportional to their actual influence.

A third reason is that in such cases the media is profiting from the misdeeds of others. In this specific case the O. J. Simpson special was to be shown on Fox during the November sweeps. This is the time when stations measure the extent of their viewership in order to set their advertising rates. The more viewers, the more they can charge for advertising. Put bluntly, the brutal murder of two people was to be exploited so that more money could be charged for advertising. It is not unreasonable to regard this sort of behaviour as making the media a party to the crime. To use an analogy, suppose that Bill robs Ted and sells the loot to Sally who then sells it at a profit to her customers. While it can be argued that Sally is not as bad as Bill, it is clear that she has bought into his crime and has committed a wrongful deed. When a media company buys a story like O. J.'s, they are buying into his crime and are committing a wrongful deed.

It might be objected that the media is just buying a product from the person and is not endorsing or condoning her crime. Hence, it can be argued that it is acceptable for the media to profit from such purchases.

It can be replied that if this objection is plausible, then the same defence can be used by people who knowingly purchase stolen goods or who otherwise benefit from the crimes of others. This sort of defence is rather lacking in plausibility. Thus, it must be concluded that the media acts wrongly when it publishes books and airs TV shows that reward those who have committed misdeeds.

The immoral secret

Australian TV producer Rhonda Byrne has told the world her secret in her book and DVD. This secret is what she calls 'the law of attraction'.[73]

According to empowerment advocate Lisa Nichols, this works in the following way: 'when you think of the things you want, and you focus on them with all your intention, then the law of attraction will give you exactly what you want, every time'. Not surprisingly, positive thoughts and feelings are rewarded. This process is illustrated in the film: a woman obsessing over a bauble in a jewellery store window soon finds the necklace around her neck – apparently with no effort on her part. In another scene, a boy visualizes himself with a new bike and it soon appears. This law apparently even helps with parking – in the film a financial consultant is able to find empty parking spaces by visualizing what he wants. While getting material goods and parking spaces is appealing, using this law can apparently also cure disease. For example, a woman in the film claims that she cured her breast cancer by positive thinking.

Of course, like a magnet, the law of attraction has a negative side along with its positive side. Those who have negative thoughts and feelings suffer ill consequences. For example, someone who frets over having her bike stolen will soon find it missing.

While the author claims that she wants to help people, her film and book are actually morally pernicious.

First, the works put forth a false account of how the world actually functions. As was argued in the Implausible Secret (above), the causal claim put forth in the law of attraction runs contrary to both empirical evidence and well-tested scientific theories. Putting forth a wildly implausible account of how the world is supposed to work is morally irresponsible because people can be harmed, perhaps even seriously, if they accept such an account. One obvious example is the case of weight control. If someone who has a serious weight problem believes that he can control his weight by using the law of attraction instead of using proper diet and exercise, then there is a very good chance that his health will be impaired. As another example, if someone believes that she can cure her breast cancer by using the law of attraction and fails to seek proper medical attention, then the results are likely to be dire.

Second, the law of attraction seems to entail that each person is responsible for whatever happens to her – good or bad. While taking responsibility is generally good, claiming that people are responsible for more than they really are accountable for can have a negative psychological impact. To use an example from the film, if someone steals your bike, then your negative thinking and feelings are to blame. To use another example, if you are overweight, it cannot be a medical condition such as diabetes – it must be your negative thoughts. If someone truly believes in the law of attraction, then when bad things happen to them, they could well be doubly harmed: once by the bad event and then again by feelings of self-blame and guilt for their failure to think positively.

Naturally, a person might wonder about truly awful things – such as the genocide in Rwanda. Given the law of attraction, it would seem that the victims of the genocide were responsible for their fate because of negative thoughts and feelings. Obviously, this would be a rather reprehensible thing to claim.

Byrne was asked about Rwanda in a telephone interview conducted by *Newsweek* (5 March 2007). Her reply was: 'If we are in fear, if we're feeling in our lives that we're victims and feeling powerless, then we are on a frequency of attracting those things to us . . . totally unconsciously, totally innocently, totally all those words that are so important.'[74]

This quote creates a bit of a problem. Like all positive-thinking people, Byrne puts forth her works as advice on what people should do in regards to their thoughts and feelings. This, naturally enough, presumes that people can control their thoughts and feelings. If people can do this, then they would seem to be responsible for their own negative thoughts and feelings. If negative thoughts and feelings of the genocide victims caused their suffering, then they are not innocent. In effect, they committed suicide by negative thoughts and feelings.

If negative thoughts and feelings are unconscious and innocent, then presumably it follows they are not under our control. If the law of attraction is correct, the victims in Rwanda caused their own deaths in the same way that a wounded and bleeding person caused a shark to attack: they simply attracted harm through no fault of their own.

However, if negative thoughts and feelings are not under our control, then it would seem that positive thoughts would also not be under our control. After all, if they were, then the genocide victims could have just thought enough positive thoughts to offset the negative thoughts and spared themselves. But, if our thoughts and feelings are not under our control, then the book and movie are pointless.

Third, the law of attraction seems to entail that people are not responsible for what they actually do. Consider, for example, the case of the person who can supposedly get a parking space by visualizing this. This entails that his thoughts control other people by somehow causing them either not to park in the spot he desires or to leave it when he is approaching. As another example, consider the cases of the necklace and the bike. Manufactured goods do not appear out of nothing, so presumably the desires of the woman and the child caused other people to bring them what they wanted. As a final example, consider the genocide in Rwanda. By Byrne's account, the negative thoughts of the victims brought their deaths and suffering to them. Under the law of attraction it would seem that people are puppets to the thoughts and feelings of other people. After all, since people are part of reality, if thoughts and feelings control reality, then they control people. Thus, when people take an action it would seem that they are not acting freely. If Sally gives Tom a Playstation 3, it would seem to be because Tom had positive thoughts and feelings about the PS3. If Sally stabs Tom in the face, then it would seem to be because Tom had negative thoughts and feelings that attracted a knife to his left eye. In any case, Sally is not responsible for her actions – Tom's feelings and thoughts are. If Tom does not control his thoughts and feelings, then he is not responsible either. In this case, no one is responsible for anything at all.

Given the above discussion, it is now no secret that *The Secret* is fraught with moral problems.

10 Animals

Although we tend to think mainly about ourselves, we share the earth with untold other species. Many of these species are facing extinction. Others that are not facing extinction are apparently too tasty for their own safety. This subsection includes a look at extinction and goose liver.

Letting species die: the case for extinction

These days, most right-thinking individuals believe species should be saved from extinction. Despite the popularity of this view, species continue to follow the dodo, the dinosaurs and disco into extinction. It is the purpose of this provocation to argue that at least some species should be allowed to die.

An easy way to support this claim would be to focus on species that are harmful and whose passing no one would mourn. For example, no one would shed a tear at the passing of tapeworms. Since this is the easy path, it will not be taken. Instead arguments will be given in support of allowing even non-harmful species to die.

The first argument for allowing species to die is based on the principle of triage. In medicine, triage is a system of categorizing victims for treatment and it is aimed at saving as many lives as possible. The lives that are saved are often saved at the cost of allowing others to die. This principle can be extended from individuals to species. While numerous species are in danger of extinction, the available resources are limited. Some species need land, but appropriate land is expensive, if it is available at all. Some species require artificial techniques even to reproduce. Other species have other needs and these needs tend to be costly. Given the scarcity of resources and the costs involved, it is impossible to save all the species that are in danger. In this case, the principle of triage must be applied and some species will have to perish so that others might live. Thus, it is acceptable to let some species die.

While the principle of triage does allow some to die in order to save others, it does not indicate who should be saved and who should be sacrificed. Not surprisingly, it can be argued that humans should be given priority. A reasonably uncontroversial argument is as follows.

It is generally accepted that a person has a special obligation to his or her own family. For example, if Jane's brother is starving, Jane should provide him with food before she gives food to a complete stranger. By analogy, humans should help other humans first before going to the aid of other species. Given the limited amount of resources, things like land, medical resources and human labour should be spent solving problems that humans face, such as poverty and starvation. Once the human problems have been solved, then resources can be spent saving non-human species. Until then, these species will simply have to wait. During this time, some species will no doubt become extinct.

It might be objected that this special obligation is unprincipled: what is it, exactly, about humans that would create such a special obligation that would not apply to other species as well?

One reply is that there is nothing special about Jane's family beyond the fact that it is her family. The same is true of humans – humans owe other humans simply because they are the same kind.

A second and controversial reply is that humans are superior to other species and hence they should receive priority. To use an analogy, when a ship is damaged and sinking, the crew focuses on repairing the most important systems first. Less important systems are repaired later if time and resources permit. Thus, some species must be allowed to pass from the earth so that humans can be saved.

It might be objected that the above arguments are mistaken because they involve matching individual humans against endangered species. It can be contended that it is the species, not the individual, that is important. While individual humans could be saved and aided by the resources that would otherwise be used to save an endangered species, humanity itself is in no immediate danger of extinction. Hence, the principle of triage would justify sacrificing some individual humans to save entire species. To use an analogy, if one patient is in danger of losing some cells that she will soon replace and another patient is about to perish completely, the doctor would be obligated to give priority to the second patient.

In reply, it must be noted that death comes to a species through the death of individuals – death is a very personal thing. Particular humans are sacrificed not to save some abstract entity ('the species') but to save particular individuals and hence it is as individual to individual that they must be compared. J. S. Mill argues in *Utilitarianism* that human capacities exceed those of animals. If this is correct, then individual humans should be chosen over individual animals. Thus it is acceptable to let some species die in order to save humans.

Two final arguments can be given for allowing species to die. Both of these arguments are based on the assumption that extinction is a natural part of life. Given the fossil record, this is a reasonable assumption.

The first argument is as follows. There is no moral obligation to save an individual from a natural death (such as old age). The individual has lived out her time and it has come to an end. By analogy, when a species becomes extinct naturally, it has lived out its time and should be allowed to die.

An obvious objection is that just as an individual can be kept alive through artificial means, a species can be kept going past the point when it 'should' have died out. In response, this objection is based on the assumption that an individual life or species should be preserved simply because it can be preserved. However, it is not mere existence that matters, but the quality and dignity of that existence. It has often been argued that individuals should be allowed to die with dignity rather than being kept alive through artificial means. The same types of arguments can be pressed into service to allow species to die. If a species has lost its ability to survive on its own and can only continue to exist through artificial means, then it no longer has a dignified existence and should be allowed to die. Ironically, people who tend to favour allowing humans to die with dignity tend to want to deny species that basic right. And people who are all too happy to allow species to pass out of existence are often against allowing humans the same opportunity.

Even if this argument is seen as effective and it is accepted that humans are not obligated to save species from natural extinction, an obvious concern is raised by the fact that humans have caused some species to become extinct. The impact of humans on the world continues and only the most foolish would claim that humans are not currently taking an active role in driving species towards extinction.

Now, if the actions of Sally needlessly put Bill into danger, then it seems quite reasonable to expect Sally to either stop such actions or at least aid Bill. The same line of reasoning, it can be argued, must be applied to species: humans are under an obligation to avoid harming species or at least to aid the species they have harmed. Thus, some species should not be allowed to die.

There are, of course, responses to this concern. First, it can be argued (again) that the needs of humans outweigh the needs of other species, at least in some cases. Hence, a utilitarian argument could be given for allowing some species to die. Some cases would be fairly uncontroversial (allowing deadly parasites to go extinct), others would be more controversial (permitting the extinction of a species of bird in order to build more housing). Such situations would have to be addressed on a case-by-case basis, but it seems reasonable to expect that at least some of the time it would be acceptable for a species to die.

As a second reply, it can be argued that some species do cause other species to go extinct, but this is part of the natural process of evolution. Humans are a natural species, therefore any species that becomes extinct due to human activities would become naturally extinct. As argued above, humans have no obligation to prevent natural extinction.

One reply to this is that humans are not natural, hence any extinctions humans might cause are not natural. Because of this, those species should not be allowed to die.

In reply, while humans seem to be as natural as any other creature, suppose that it is true that humans are somehow distinct from all other natural creatures. It is reasonable to think that this would lay the foundation for an argument in support of human superiority. And if humans are superior, this would certainly seem to justify allowing a species to go extinct if such extinction would benefit humans. Clearly, placing humans outside of nature would not be an effective objection.

Another objection is that while humans are natural and part of the natural process of evolution, humans have a capacity for destruction that far exceeds those of other species. And, most importantly, humans can decide whether or not to engage in such activities. Since humans have this choice, any extinction caused by humans is different from other types of extinction. This difference, it can be argued, is morally relevant and provides the basis for arguing that humans should not choose to allow species to die.

This is a reasonable concern and it seems almost obvious that humans should not callously or casually permit species to die. However, if Darwin is right, then all species are involved in the struggle he mentions and this struggle will inevitably result in the extinction of some species. This is true of all species, including humans. Because of this, there will be some species that go extinct simply because humans exist and despite the best intentions of humanity. This sort of inevitable extinction seems perfectly acceptable and thus such species should be allowed to die.

In the face of the above arguments it seems reasonable that some species should be allowed to die. But it must be noted that these arguments do not entail that humans should have a free hand in eradicating species even when doing so might be beneficial to humanity.

Foie gras and philosophy

Many feathers have been ruffled recently in the moral debate over foie gras. For those not familiar with this food, it is the swollen liver of a goose or duck. This swollen state is produced by force-feeding the bird via a tube – certainly not a pleasant experience for the animal. Not surprisingly, animal rights activists tend to find this sort of thing morally appalling. Those with a more gastronomic inclination tend to regard it as acceptable and even very tasty.

The debate over the morality of mistreating animals and eating them is clearly philosophically interesting. However, this situation also raises another matter of concern: this debate has clearly revealed that philosophical ignorance is rather widespread among those discussing the matter. This ignorance, one may safely assume, probably extends beyond this issue. A *Newsweek* article, 'A Flap Over Foie Gras', (2 May 2005) nicely reveals the nature of the ignorance.

First, consider the position of American-French chef Rick Tramonto. In response to Chef Charlie Trotter's decision to stop serving foie gras (but to keep serving other meat dishes), chef Tramonto said 'Either you eat animals or you don't eat animals.'[75] While this is a good example of a tautology (a claim that is true in virtue of its logical structure), it also nicely expresses the fallacy known as false dilemma. The idea is that a person present two alternatives, rejects one and then asserts that the remaining one must be correct. This reasoning is fallacious when there are, in fact, more than two alternatives – both of the presented alternatives could be incorrect/false, while a third (or twentieth) alternative is correct/true.

While it is true that one either does or does not eat animals, there certainly are many alternatives lying between not eating animals at all and eating any animal. To use an analogy, consider the case of killing. While it is true that a person either kills or does not kill, there are moral distinctions in killing. Intuitively, a person who kills for fun and thrills is doing something wrong. A person who has killed another person because it was absolutely necessary to protect the innocent is a killer, but certainly is morally distinct from the thrill killer. Thus, a person can reject thrill killing on ethical grounds, yet still find killing in self-defence morally acceptable.

Likewise, there seem to be moral distinctions in the realm of eating animals. For example, someone who slowly cooks dogs alive because 'they taste better that way' certainly seems morally worse than someone who kills a partridge with a quick shot and then cooks it for dinner. Given that such moral distinctions can be made, someone can reject foie gras on ethical grounds and still continue to eat or serve other meat dishes. Chef Trotter might be wrong – but if he is, the mistake does not lie in deciding to take a more complex position than 'all or nothing'.

Second, consider the (alleged) activities of anti-foie gras activists. Laurent Manrique reported that his specialty food store (which sells foie gras) was vandalized and that he was sent a video showing him and his family eating dinner at home. The tape was presumably a threat – such video tapes are a known method for sending the threatening message 'we know where you live'.[76]

If it is assumed that the anti-foie gras activists (allegedly) involved in these activities oppose foie gras on the moral ground that harming animals is wrong, then it can be concluded that they are in need of philosophical education. After all, if foie gras is wrong because of the suffering of the birds, then it would seem to follow that harming humans is wrong as well. To be morally consistent, these supposed activists would need to use activities of greater moral respectability – such as openly presenting their dissent without resorting to the tactics of thugs and cowards.

Of course, the above assumes that the activists are motivated by a moral commitment to oppose harm. It might be the case that they are operating on other moral principles or that their motivation is something else entirely – perhaps they simply enjoy threatening people and pretending they are morally motivated. If it is the latter, then they could certainly benefit from philosophical training and, perhaps, therapy.

Finally, consider the 'arguments' presented by Michael Ginor and Jacques Pepin. Michael Ginor, an owner of the largest American foie gras farm, responds to the moral attacks on foie gras by pointing out that 'it's been around for 5,000 years'. Jacques Pepin, presented by *Newsweek* as 'author, teacher', stated that 'Foie gras has been around for thousands of years. If we've been doing something for so long, it can't be so bad.'[77]

Given this statement, one must hope that Jacques Pepin is not a logic teacher – his statement is a clear example of the fallacy known as appeal to tradition. This fallacy occurs when it is assumed that something is correct simply because it is traditional or 'always has been done'.

This sort of 'reasoning' is fallacious because the fact that a practice is traditional or long-standing does not establish that it is correct or acceptable. Given the reasoning used by Ginor and Pepin, slavery, war, genocide, murder, rape, torture and theft would all be morally acceptable. They all have, after all, been around for more than 5,000 years. Intuitively, all these things seem to be rather bad. So, it seems quite reasonable to hold that humans could have been doing some rather bad things, perhaps including making foie gras, for quite some time. Thus, this 'argument' in favour of foie gras fails.

Interestingly, while the authors of the *Newsweek* article did express their opinion on the matter ('Its texture as meltingly soft as a choco-late truffle, its flavor a mouth-filling meatiness and sweetness that helps justify humanity's million year struggle to the top of the food chain'),[78] they offered no comments on the fallacious reasoning on the part of the participants in the debate. Of course, it might be claimed that articles (as opposed to editorials) in a news magazine should simply report facts and not assess. In response, I have two claims. First, the authors (as most reporters do these days) did make their own opinion clear, thus removing any claim to being impartial conveyors of facts. Second, simply presenting 'the facts' to readers is not enough. Just as sources should be clearly identified, the quality of the arguments should also be indicated to the reader, using tested methods of logic. After all, if an argument is a blatant fallacy, a mag-azine does the readers a disservice by presenting it without noting that fact. I even suspect that this failure contributes to the spread of poor reasoning. What about foie gras? Never touch the stuff myself . . . it is, after all, still liver.

11   Art and Ethics

When I was a graduate student, my friends and I mocked the 'cigarette and beret crowd' who did aesthetics. Imagine my horror when I was assigned to teach the aesthetics class when I was hired at Florida A&M University. Although I do not smoke and I am still beret-free, I have written about artistic violence and the rights of artists (or lack thereof).

Lights, camera, blood

Violence is an ever-increasing part of both the real world and the fictional worlds of cinema. Hence, it is not surprising that some suspect there is a connection between the two. While few, if any, people go so far as to claim that the violence in films such as *Reservoir Dogs* and *The Matrix* is the main cause of violent behaviour in the real world, many do claim that cinematic violence does contribute to the creation of real violence.

While belief in a connection between fictional and real violence has generated many strident calls for censorship and numerous emotional appeals against violence in films, reasonable arguments against cinematic violence can be presented. Naturally, arguments for censorship are often met with strident calls for artistic freedom and emotional appeals against interference with the arts.

My objective is to avoid all strident calls and emotional appeals. Instead, I will present a reasonable case for censoring cinematic violence and then make use of this case to present an even more reasonable case for including violence in films.

The philosophic discussion of the effect of art on people is a rather old one and dates at least as far back as Plato. In the *Republic*[79] Plato argued for the censorship of poetry based on its corrupting effect on the human soul. In the *Poetics*, his pupil Aristotle claimed that people like art because they learn from it. The idea that art can have a corrupting effect and an educational aspect serves as the inspiration for the arguments that follow.

It can be argued that cinematic violence should be censored in order to reduce the occurrence of certain types of real violence. Two arguments will be presented for this claim.

First, repeated exposure to the sounds and images of cinematic violence can teach or condition a person to accept such sounds and images as normal. After all, what counts as normal for a person is, at least in part, set by what he or she regularly experiences. If violence, even cinematic violence, becomes a 'normal' part of a person's life, it is easy to see how she might become desensitized to violence. This 'corruption' can lower a person's 'violence threshold' so that it is easier for the person to engage in violence.

By censoring cinematic violence it is possible to reduce exposure to such violent images and sounds, thus decreasing the chances that people will become desensitized to violence.

Second, the curriculum of cinematic violence often includes the lesson that violence is an effective and acceptable solution to problems. Films such as *The Replacement Killers*, *The Matrix* and *Lethal Weapon 4* seem to show the viewer that problems are best dealt with by killing other people and destroying things.

While it is extremely unlikely that cinematic violence can directly cause a person to re-create scenes from a film to 'solve' his problems, it does seem reasonable to believe that a person can be taught to see such cinematic solutions as viable options for real life. This is especially true when a person is not exposed to other options for solving problems.

Curtailing cinematic violence can reduce the likelihood that people, especially children and young adults, will be taught the lesson that violence is a viable solution to life's problems. Thus, it seems reasonable to censor cinematic violence.

While these arguments seem reasonable, a more reasonable case can be made for keeping violence as an element in films. This case is as follows.

If the portrayal of violence in films has no effect on people, then there is clearly no reason to attempt to combat such violence on moral grounds. There could be, of course, reasons to oppose the violence on aesthetic grounds, but such a discussion goes beyond the scope of this work.

However, if the portrayal of violence in films is powerful enough to have a negative effect on a person's character and teach people to engage in real violence, then, as has been argued, it might be reasonable to simply remove the violence from cinema. However, this would be wasting an excellent opportunity. If cinematic violence can affect people in a negative manner, it seems reasonable to believe that, perhaps paradoxically, violence can be used to affect people in a positive manner.

As noted above, in the *Poetics* Aristotle claims that people like art because they are at the same time learning. Interestingly enough, Aristotle's remarks about the educational nature of art took place within his discussion of tragedy. It is contended that cinematic tragedy does have something to teach people.

According to the generally accepted definition, tragedy involves the main character going from a state of happiness to a state of misery. It is contended that this transition is best brought about through violence.

Psychologically, most people fear violence. This is because no one, as Socrates said in the *Apology*, wants to be harmed. Seeing violence, even fictional violence, inflicted on a person typically creates pity in normal people. Since violence has such a profound psychological effect on people, and tragedy aims at creating pity and fear in the audience, it seems that violence is a suitable, even ideal, means of creating this effect. In fact, it would be difficult to imagine a true tragedy without some kind of violence.

The audience is, of course, supposed to feel pity and fear. Pity and fear certainly seem to be proper and right responses to tragic violence. Tragic violence in films can teach that violence is something to fear and that those who suffer it should be pitied. People who learn this lesson would probably be less likely to engage in violence. Because of this lesson, it would be a mistake to censor tragic violence in films such as *Romeo and Juliet* and especially films that dramatize real-life tragedies, such as *Malcolm X*.

Of course, it can be countered that even if tragic violence is acceptable, even laudable, other types of violent films should still be censored. However, the specific argument used to justify tragic violence in films can be expanded to justify violence in films that are not tragedies. This expanded argument is as follows.

While tragedy is one of the most effective ways of teaching what might be called the proper lesson about violence, other types of films can teach similar lessons. Films that fit into this category are those that clearly show that violence is a nasty business that leads to pain, loss and suffering. These films stand in contrast to films that teach that violence is glorious, without serious consequences, or is a desirable solution to problems. *Saving Private Ryan* is a good example of a film that shows violence for what it really is. Other examples include various 'social commentary' films, especially those that directly address the topic of violence.

If art does, in fact, have a powerful psychological effect on people, then such films can be used to teach people that violence is a terrible thing. Teaching this lesson could certainly have a greater effect on people than simply purging violence from films. After all, a positive lesson or influence is certainly better than the absence of a lesson or influence. The lessons taught by such films can have an uplifting, as opposed to corrupting, influence on the character and teach the lesson that violence is not glorious and not a reasonable solution to life's problems. Thus, as long as a film's portrayal of violence has a positive lesson or at least does not have a corrupting influence, then there would be no moral justification for censoring the violence in the film.

While the arguments just presented are against censorship, some people who oppose censorship might find them less than satisfying for at least two reasons. First, these arguments clearly rest on the assumption that the arts should teach a moral lesson or at least avoid corrupting people. Those who believe that art is above such moral concerns or that aesthetic factors can outweigh moral concerns will, of course, find these arguments less than pleasing. Second, these arguments only serve to protect a very limited set of films from censorship.

Since a majority of modern films that contain violence do not fall within this set, it seems reasonable to be concerned that the arguments do not go far enough.

To address these two concerns, one final argument will be presented. This is the aesthetic argument for necessary violence that is as follows.

In the *Poetics* Aristotle[80] claims that a work is flawed if it contains elements that are not plausible. This is a reasonable aesthetic standard. After all, films that lack the right sort of plausibility will not be convincing to the audience and hence the members of the audience will not be able to suspend their disbelief and become involved in and affected by the film. Clearly, a film that fails to engage the audience would be a flawed work from an aesthetic standpoint.

Experience shows that many significant, powerful and interesting events involve violence. These events include such things as crimes, assassinations, intense personal conflict, social upheaval, revolution and war. To avoid portraying violence in films, filmmakers would either have to avoid such things entirely or present them in a 'sanitized' manner. Not surprisingly, examples of 'sanitized' violence abound in films aimed at children. Guns are fired with wild abandon, but bullets only damage physical objects. Cars flip and crash, but the driver and passengers walk away without a scratch. Huge explosions merely toss people to safe landings. People fall from high places, but land safely.

The first option is unreasonable. Leaving out such events when they actually should be present would create implausible and unrealistic works. For example, try to imagine films like *Saving Private Ryan*, *Apocalypse Now* and *Thin Red Line* with all the violence removed. Without the violence, these powerful films would lose most of their power and would instead seem extremely unrealistic.

While excess and gratuitous violence is certainly undesirable, the second option is also unreasonable. First, 'sanitizing' violence is still unrealistic, can lessen the power of a film, and can even make the work appear silly. Second, if art can have a powerful psychological effect on people, 'sanitized' violence could have negative consequences. The message that is sent by 'sanitized' violence seems to be that violence does not have any serious consequences and that it is often something funny. Thus, if art does have a very powerful effect on people, it would be better to show the real consequences of violence than sanitizing violence.

Thus, it would seem that violence should not be censored.

Artists' rights

Artists often claim to have a special relationship with their art that gives them rights over it even after it has been sold. This view recently created a conflict between artist David Phillips and the investment company Fidelity. Fidelity hired Phillips to create a sculpture park, but when it was completed, the company wanted to change the location of one sculpture and alter one path. Neither party was willing to compromise so Phillips sued Fidelity on the grounds that the changes would mutilate his work.[81]

Phillips' situation is nothing new. In 1958 the owner of the mobile Pittsburgh donated it to Pennsylvania's Allegheny County. Alexander Calder, the creator, objected when he learned that the black and white mobile would be repainted green and gold. Despite his objection, the mobile was repainted.[82]

In 1969 the sculptor Takis (Panayotis Vassilakis) attempted to remove his work from New York City's Museum of Modern Art.[83] He contended that, as an artist, he possessed the right to determine how his art was exhibited. He also claimed that, as the artist, he retained this right even if the work had been sold.

While the courts will resolve the legal issues, these situations raise an interesting philosophic problem regarding the rights of artists and their works.

If an artist elects to sell her work, it seems reasonable to regard the art as any other commodity or service. This claim is supported by the following.

Suppose Sally hires Jane to paint the interior of her house. After the work is done, Sally decides she has changed her mind about one room and plans to repaint it. Imagine Jane learns of this and demands the room be left unchanged. Imagine further that Sally learns that Jane intends to spend her painting fee on a new laptop and demands that Jane give the money to charity instead. While Sally's demand might seem absurd, it is no more absurd than Jane's demand – either both have a right to control their former property or neither does. Thus, it seems reasonable to see this situation as a change of ownership and hence a change of control: Sally now owns Jane's painting and Jane now owns Sally's money. Thus, neither has a right to tell the other what she can or cannot do with her new property.

If the analogy holds, an artist who wishes to retain the right to control his work must place such restrictions in the original agreement (or not sell it at all). To simply insist on new conditions after the sale would be unfair.

It might be objected that the artist has a special relationship with his art that places it outside the 'commercial' realm and that this gives an artist the right to control his work even after selling it. In reply, when the artist agrees to sell his work for money, he places the art within the 'commercial' realm. He cannot consistently accept payment and at the same time insist that art is special – he cannot have his cake and eat it too. This point can be further illustrated by an analogy to marriage.

When two people are married, a special relationship exists giving each certain rights others do not possess. For example, only the wife has the right to have sexual relations with the husband. Given this, the wife has a right to control her husband's sexual activities. By analogy, the artist can claim a right to control her work via a special relationship that exists between them.

Continuing the analogy, if the wife treats her husband like a prostitute ('selling' him to other women), then she can no longer expect to have a special right to control his sexual activities. If she wanted the special relationship to continue, she should not have taken the money. The same is true regarding art: if the artist wants to keep the special relationship intact, she should not prostitute her art by selling it.

It might be claimed that a work of art itself has an inherent right not be altered. In reply, it can be claimed that a work of art does not intuitively seem to be an entity that can have rights. While it is reasonable to suppose that people and animals have rights, it seems odd to assert that a non-sentient thing has rights. After all, rights against abuse are often based on the fact that the thing in question can suffer, and while art might cause suffering, it is clear that art cannot suffer. Thus, the burden of proof would seem to rest on those who claim that a work of art has such a right.

Thus, if an artist treats her work as a commodity to be sold, she should accept that the purchaser has every right to treat it the same way.

12   Philosophers, Atheists, Choosers and Frauds

This section provides an assortment of moral issues. The perennial favourite of God and ethics is addressed, as is the badness of choice and fraud in science. Also addressed is the question of whether philosophers are immoral or not.

Immoral philosophers?

Imagine, if you will, a once noble vessel, now stricken and adrift. Many of the decks are ruined shells, filled with debris and inhabited by the lost and helpless. Other decks are nicer, but still plagued with troubles. To make matters worse, members of the crew and passengers live in rival groups and periodically slaughter each other over various matters. The situation is all the more hopeless because there are no lifeboats and virtually no chance of any outside help (although some swear to have seen lights in the sky).

Some few do try to set the ship right and get her back on course. Oddly enough, some of the brightest passengers have retreated into the ship's towers (the walls of which are lined with tiles of finely cut elephant tusks). In the towers, these bright people scribble furiously on scraps of paper in languages only they and their fellows can understand. These scraps, which deal with such dire matters as whether blue is green or green is blue, are passed from tower to tower to the delight of the inhabitants. Sometimes they gather together in bands and, behind tightly closed doors, discuss important matters such as whether they exist or not. While one might expect the crew and passengers would unite and toss such oddballs to the sharks, they do not. Instead, regular tribute is given to the tower dwellers.

Given the dire plight of the ship, it seems immoral for the tower dwellers to squander their intellects and the ship's resources in such activities. Instead, it seems fair to expect them to help solve the problems that plague the stricken vessel, and those on board.

Not surprisingly, the stricken ship is a crudely obvious metaphor for the earth and the 'oddballs' in the tower are, of course, philosophers.

While the analogy might seem a bit silly, it is not all that far from the truth. After all, one has but to look at the daily paper or any news show to see just how well things are going. War, crime, disease, sexism, racism, violence, genocide and other problems abound in the 'real' world.

Philosophers are often regarded as being detached from the 'real' world. This is shown, in part, by the fact that philosophers tend to focus on highly abstract, often self-generated puzzles and conundrums whose solutions (if ever obtained) would seem to have no significant consequences. Further, even when philosophers attempt to address 'real' problems, they seem to take perverse delight in creating the most diabolically convoluted and irrelevant papers and presentations possible. Naturally, these papers and presentations are largely for the consumption of other philosophers.

Additionally, philosophers are conspicuously (but not entirely) absent from the media, political debates, primary schools, secondary schools and other places outside of the ivory towers of academics.

Thus, it would seem that philosophers are all too similar to the 'oddballs' on the stricken ship. Given that the 'oddballs' seem to be immoral, it would seem that philosophers are immoral as well.

Perhaps philosophers can be defended from this charge. The charge of immorality can only stick if philosophers are actually morally obligated to become involved in the problems of the 'real world'.

Now, it might be thought that this provocation is begging the question by simply assuming that such an obligation exists. However, the analogy of the stricken ship counters this. When people are on a stricken vessel, each person is expected to help out with the situation unless they have a reasonable excuse that limits or eliminates their responsibility. It seems reasonable to take the current situation on earth to be remarkably like that of a stricken ship. Thus, philosophers are under an obligation to help out. So the discussion now turns to the matter of determining whether philosophers have a reasonable excuse or not.

On a stricken ship, people might be excused from helping if they are ignorant of the plight of the ship, if they are incapable of helping, if the danger is too great, or if they are doing something more important. The same excuses might be offered in defence of the philosophers.

Philosophers might claim that they are ignorant of the problems in question. If this were true, the philosophers could be excused. This would be analogous to excusing passengers who, out of ignorance of the plight, kept playing cards and drinking while their ship was sinking. While philosophers often claim to be sceptics and to 'know nothing', a philosopher would truly have to spend all her time in a cave to maintain ignorance of the problems that take place daily. Thus, ignorance would seem to be no excuse for most philosophers.

Philosophers might claim that they are incapable of helping. If philosophers could not help, then they would not, of course, be obligated to attempt to do so. Using the ship analogy, infants and severely injured people are excused from helping, because they lack the capacity to assist. While most philosophers are not up to strenuous physical tasks, virtually every problem confronting people today has at least some aspect that requires thought and logical problem solving. Philosophers could, of course, assert that they lack the intellectual and logical abilities to confront such problems. However, given that philosophers pride themselves on their intellectual prowess and problem-solving abilities, this path does not seem to be a viable one. In fact, the possession of such finely honed mental abilities creates an even greater obligation for philosophers. By analogy, an extremely strong, healthy and skilled sailor would be regarded as being that much more obligated to help out with the plight of the ship. If he simply stood idly by while people drowned, he would be regarded as all the more villainous because of her capabilities. Thus, it would seem that philosophers could not be excused because of a lack of abilities.

Philosophers might claim that the danger of involvement is too great. To use the ship analogy, people are not expected to put themselves at great risk, even to rescue others. Philosophers can point to the fate of Socrates. He became actively involved in the affairs of his community and was given a nice cup of hemlock for his troubles. It would be unreasonable, they might argue, for a philosopher to risk such a fate. While this would be a reasonable reply for philosophers living in dangerous countries, most philosophers live in places that have laws that prevent philosophers from being put to death (or even charged at all) for such 'crimes'. Such philosophers could argue that becoming involved in 'real' problems could doom their careers as professional philosophers. They could become branded as 'pop' philosophers and end up being laughed out of the ivory towers. While this reply does have some merit (this is actually a real risk), the 'pop' philosopher charge only has validity if the 'real' problems have less merit than the 'philosophical' problems. It is to this matter that the discussion now turns.

The last defence of philosophers is that they are doing something more important and hence are excused from involvement. To continue with the ship analogy, a doctor struggling to save the life of a patient would be excused from helping passengers into the lifeboats because her task is more important. The same might be said of the work of philosophers. Since at least the time of Plato, philosophers have regarded themselves as being involved with the truly important problems, with the real world. Other people, to use Plato's metaphor, are living in dark caves and playing with mere illusions. If this is true, then it is not the philosophers who are in the wrong. Rather, it is everyone else, for they are simply wasting their lives, resources and energy on illusions and pseudo-problems.

This reply, as noted, has a very distinct pedigree and a long and noble lineage. There is also some truth to the matter. Many philosophic problems are rightly regarded as very important matters and some are even regarded as eternal and essential questions. Bertrand Russell, in *The Problems of Philosophy*,[84] presents an eloquent and excellent case for the value of philosophy and philosophic questions. To blend Russell's words with a wonderful line from *The Matrix*, it's the questions that drive us to expand our imaginations, to open up new possibilities and to free ourselves from dogmatism. These things certainly seem good and worthwhile.

While Russell argued for the value of philosophy, he also recognized the importance of being involved in the problems of the 'real' world. Perhaps the best example of this was in 1960 when Russell told a journalist that there was no time to talk about philosophy in the face of the nuclear threat. True to his word, Russell went out and was arrested for protesting against nuclear weapons. Thus, it would seem that philosophers are not excused from being involved in 'real' world problems. Of course, such an argument from authority is relatively weak. Fortunately, another argument can be given.

If philosophers defend their pursuits by claiming that the importance of the philosophic problems obligates them to work on them, then it would seem that philosophers would be equally obligated to work on problems of similar importance. It seems reasonable that matters of life and death, the survival of the human race, and human freedom are matters which are equally important as the problem of personal identity, epistemology and whether beauty is a real quality of objects or not. Hence, it would seem that philosophers cannot be excused simply by claiming that what they do is too important to allow the 'real' world to interfere. This does not mean that philosophers should stop doing philosophy. Many philosophic questions overlap with and are relevant to critical 'real' world problems. And, as noted above, philosophers are actually ideally suited to deal with problems in a rational and logical manner.

Thus, philosophers should still do philosophy, but they should also become more involved in the problems of the world.

It might be objected that philosophers are being cut from the general herd of professional academics and given an unfair branding. While the criticism raised in this work can be brought against virtually all academic disciplines, the criticism is most telling against philosophers. There are four reasons to believe this. First, philosophers pride themselves on being 'lovers of wisdom'. Because wisdom is essential for dealing with problems, the wise are under a special obligation to deal with such problems. Second, philosophers already work on many 'real world' problems on an abstract level. Hence, they are better qualified than many other academics to work on many such problems (such as critical ethical issues). Because of this greater ability, they would have a greater obligation. Third, ethics is a domain of philosophy. Since the argument is a moral one, it should be most effective on those who do ethics, namely philosophers. Finally, philosophy is the most general field of 'problem solving'. Virtually any problem can be recast as a philosophic problem. This is not true of other disciplines. For example, one would be hard pressed to recast the ethical quandaries of the human genome project as mathematical problems or matters for art historians. Hence, philosophers are 'intellectually responsible' for a broader range of problems than other academics, and this responsibility extends to the problems of the real world.

God, ethics and atheism

Humans generally regard murder and theft as wrong while universally praising kindness, charity and honesty. One problem in ethics is determining the basis for these common moral intuitions. As a solution, some have proposed a set of universal moral laws known, however dimly, by humans.

While some claim that the moral laws are fundamentally connected with God, others propose non-religious accounts. While the latest fad involves evolutionary accounts of ethics, non-religious ethics is nothing new. Thinkers ranging from Aristotle to Kant have proposed such theories.

A recent book discussing God, evolution and ethics is Richard Dawkins' *The God Delusion*.[85] Pursuing the stock evolutionary line, he claims that morality arose from natural selection. Simply put, the engine of evolution is driven by survival and the propagation of the genes. While altruistic behaviour, such as taking risks to aid others, might seem contrary to natural selection, he attempts an explanation. He notes that seemingly altruistic actions might involve aiding genetic relatives. Further, altruistic acts might create goodwill or a reputation that would help future mating chances. Of course, some humans perform acts of altruism that seem to have no chance of yielding such evolutionary payoffs. For example, people anonymously aid strangers a continent away and sometimes die trying to save strangers. Dawkins' reply is that altruistic tendencies must have evolved when humans lived in small, closely related groups. Though most humans now live in large groups, these behavioural tendencies remain and incline altruistic behaviour even towards strangers.

Another problem in ethics is providing an answer to the question 'why be good?' As Dawkins notes, those who accept a religious-based ethics can provide a pragmatic answer: be good to avoid God's punishments and to receive his rewards. For Dawkins, this is not a moral reply, but mere 'sucking up'.[86]

On one hand, it is tempting to assume that the evolutionary accounts of ethics do not need to answer the question 'why be moral?' After all, they are presented to explain behaviour rather than provide moral prescriptions. If morality, like the ear, arose from natural selection, then asking 'why be moral?' makes as much sense as asking 'why hear sounds?' Organisms simply do what they do.

On the other hand, it seems fair to consider what answer can be given to this question within the context of the evolutionary account. In short: why be good if morality is only a behavioural strategy that arose via natural selection?

An obvious reply is that one should be moral because doing so will increase the chances of passing on one's genes. This reply is not without its problems.

One obvious problem is that if the reason to be good is based on reproduction, then those who do not wish to reproduce will have no reason to be good.

A second problem arises because the reason to be moral is based on achieving a goal. From a rational standpoint, if this goal can be achieved using an alternative approach that was easier and more desirable, then the motivation to be moral would vanish.

Interestingly, being moral is generally regarded as difficult and undesirable. In contrast, not being moral is generally seen as easier and desirable. That this is so is supported by the fact that the problem in ethics is to answer the question 'why be good?' This indicates that people need a reason to be good and prefer not being good. This view is further supported by Glaucon's argument. In Plato's *Republic*[87] he presents an eloquent account of how people are moral only against their will and that being unjust is vastly preferable to being just. Of course, as Glaucon points out, there are excellent reasons to appear to be moral. Doing so enables one to conceal one's misdeeds (and thus avoid punishment) and permits one to enjoy the rewards of a good reputation. Thus, appearing to be good enables one to enjoy the best of both worlds: one can enjoy the ease and freedom of being unrestricted by moral limits while enjoying the benefits of a good, albeit false, reputation. Thus, there would seem to be no reason to actually be moral if the evolutionary account is true.

One might object that most people are not up to the task of faking goodness. For such incompetent people there are two excellent reasons to be good. First, the reward: being good would boost their reproductive chances. Second, the avoidance of harms: being good would help them avoid being punished for misdeeds. But this does not seem to be a moral reply. After all, as Dawkins claims, being good to get rewards and avoid harms is just 'sucking up'. Thus, it seems that the evolutionary account is no better at providing a moral reply than the religious account to this ancient question.

Is choice bad?

While philosophy is often regarded as trailing the sciences, the reverse is often the case. One case is the connection between freedom and happiness. While philosophers have often discussed the connection between them, it is probably the existentialists, such as Jean-Paul Sartre, who have focused the most attention on this matter.

A key tenet in Sartre's existentialism is that anguish follows a person's realization that she is free to select from a multitude of available choices.[88] Confronted with such freedom, people try to impose order but end up failing. In their failure they become miserable.

Interestingly enough, Sartre's view of the connection between choice and unhappiness seems to have been confirmed by social scientists such as Robert E. Lane, David G. Myers and Barry Schwartz.[89]

Schwartz and his fellows divide people into two categories based on their approaches: 'maximizers' (people who try to make the best choice) and 'satisficers' (people who are satisfied with making choices that are adequate).

Not surprisingly, they found maximizers spend more time than satisficers considering matters before and after making a decision (such as what computer to buy).

What is surprising is that a person's happiness tends to be inversely proportional to his maximizing tendencies. Hence, those with the highest tendency to maximize were very depressed. This seems to be the opposite of what one would expect, namely that a person who focuses more on making a better decision should be happier.

The researchers explained this in terms of various factors. First, the more choices a person is aware of, the higher opportunity cost they pay. Put briefly, when a person chooses one option they miss out on what the other options offered. Hence, the more choices a person is aware of, the greater their regret will be. Second, there is the matter of adaptation. Put roughly, the things one acquires bring less joy the longer they are owned. Because of this, the more effort a person put into making the decision to acquire a thing, the worse they will feel as it becomes less satisfying. This feeling is even worse if the person expected more in the first place. After all, the more one expects, the greater the pain will be if one gets less.

Given the results of the investigation, Schwartz infers a link between an increase in the number of choices available and unhappiness, at least in affluent countries.

As a solution, Schwartz suggests taking steps to limit the available choices. He suggests that those who offer choices, such as governments and companies, should rethink their approach. For example, he points out that when software companies write highly customizable software, the result is often more complexity and confusion (and presumably greater unhappiness).

The second part of his solution is an approach suggested centuries ago by the Stoics, most notably in Epictetus' *Enchiridion*.[90] Perhaps not realizing that he is rediscovering stoicism, Schwartz recommends that people should reduce the number of choices they make, learn to settle for what is adequate for their needs, learn not to be so concerned about what they could have had, and to lower their expectations.

While the Stoic solution is appealing, it is interesting to note that the researchers, like most social scientists, focus primarily on choices that are predominantly economic in character. Most of the examples of choice they present involve choosing one product rather than another (such as a Lexus over another car or one bottle of wine rather than another). Further, most of the studies, such as those conducted by Lyle Brenner, involve such economic matters as having people put dollar values on magazine subscriptions and flights or having them choose between money and a pen as a 'reward' for filling out a 'fake' questionnaire.

In general, social scientists should certainly not be faulted for focusing mostly on economic matters when examining the connection between choice and unhappiness. After all, economic concerns are also the main focus of most people living in affluent societies and they tend to equate happiness with economic factors.

However, social scientists should consider another theme in philosophy, one that dates back at least to Plato: happiness is not to be had by acquiring material goods. This philosophic approach suggests an alternative explanation as to why maximizers tend to be unhappier than other people. The explanation is as follows.

Given that the research tends to involve a focus on economic matters, it is reasonable to conclude that people classified by such research as maximizers are primarily economic maximizers. In other words, they would tend to be people who are interested in getting more economic or material value for their efforts. Given this, a person would tend to be focused on material goods to the degree she is a maximizer. Hence, those found to be the most concerned with maximization would tend to be most concerned with material goods. For example, they would be very concerned with having the highest-paying job, the best car, the best bottle of wine, the best deal on a flight, and so on.

As noted above, those most concerned with maximization are the unhappiest. A reasonable explanation is that they are expending the most time and energy to acquire material goods and these things cannot give them a true and lasting happiness. Given this expenditure, they have less time and energy for what would actually make them happy – hence they are significantly less happy than other people.

Thus, it is quite reasonable to suspect the maximizers are not unhappy because they have too many choices. Rather, their unhappiness lies in what they choose to value most.

Fraud, science and ethics

While science is burdened by the stereotype of the mad scientist who threatens humanity, it also enjoys the stereotype that presents the scientist as the objective and dispassionate seeker and conveyer of truth. While it is fortunate that the first stereotype rarely holds true, recent events have shown that the second one often fails to hold as well.

In the summer of 2002 the world learned that two physicists had apparently committed fraud in their research.[91] Jan Hendrik Schön, formerly of Bell Laboratories, was the main author of several impressive papers that suggested a new means of creating transistors. Unfortunately, attempts to reproduce his results failed and investigators noticed that he had apparently altered his data. The second physicist, Victor Ninov, asserted in 1999 that he and his fellow researchers had found the nuclei of elements 116 and 118. However, other researchers were unable to verify his findings and he was eventually dismissed from the Lawrence Berkeley National Laboratory.

These problems are not unique to physics. As Nicholas H. Steneck[92] of the University of Michigan notes, biologists had similar problems in the 1980s. Biologists of that time claimed that the existing system worked at uncovering fraud, but they were mistaken. Steneck implies that the same might be true of physicists.

One of the responses to the problems that arose in biology was the creation of guidelines indicating what constituted responsible behaviour – in other words, ethics for research. The effectiveness of such guidelines would depend, in part, on the willingness of the researchers to abide by such moral restrictions.

While such guidelines might be useful, it seems obvious that a researcher should not need guidelines to tell her that committing research fraud is both unprofessional and immoral. Thus, such behaviour does not seem to stem from ignorance but from a lack of willingness to do what is right.

There are numerous reasons why researchers might elect to engage in such apparently immoral behaviour. First, there is the pragmatic reason – the field of science is extremely competitive. There are only so many grants, choice positions and Nobel Prizes to go around. It is thus no surprise that this 'combat of wits', as Hobbes[93] would put it, leads to such behaviour. After all, as Glaucon argued in the *Republic*, all organisms are motivated by a desire for 'undue gain', and if anyone can gain an advantage by unjust behaviour, he would be a fool not to do so. Second, modern science itself has a tendency to undercut morality. Noted thinker Richard Dawkins argued in *The Blind Watchmaker* that the universe is devoid of not only design and purpose but also good and evil.[94] Assuming that this characterizes the scientific view of the universe, it would be odd to expect scientists to regard morality in general and moral guidelines in particular as having any foundation. One might as well expect them to believe in phlogiston.

But perhaps morality can be made scientific. Various thinkers, including Dawkins, have claimed that morality is a product of natural selection. Put very crudely, morality is an evolutionary strategy and successful moralities are those that enable genes to be passed on. On this view, there is nothing metaphysical about morality – it is grounded in the cold, hard and pitiless reality of biology and survival. Thus, it might be contended, here is a morality that scientists can accept. Problem solved, or so it seems.

Suppose a scientist realizes she has a chance to commit fraud that will potentially be of great benefit to her career. As a scientist, she realizes that her morality, just like her opposable thumb, has been a product of natural selection. She also realizes that morality, like her opposable thumb, has probably helped contribute to human survival (and thus the perpetuation of certain genes). She will almost certainly realize that none of this gives her a reason not to commit fraud. She might even consider the possibility that those who cling to morality will go the way of the large dinosaurs – successful once, but no longer so in a new age in which morality is no longer a viable strategy.

What, then, can be done? To charge the scientist with 'immorality' simply amounts to accusing her of not following a particular evolutionary strategy. She might as well be taken to task for deciding not to use her opposable thumbs. Fortunately, there is a classic method to fall back on, namely the 'morality' advocated by Glaucon in the *Republic*[95] and later by Thomas Hobbes.[96] While each scientist might wish to get away with fraud, they do not want others to get away with it. Because, of course, if fraud were rampant, the system would collapse and no one would be able to reap any plum positions or Nobel Prizes. Thus, they can make agreements not to commit fraud and can solemnly swear to punish those who decide to violate these agreements, which they regard as just. Of course, there is still that apparently eternally lingering problem of how to motivate those who think they can avoid detection or punishment . . . but I'm sure the scientists will come up with an answer to that.

13   Political and Social Thought

In addition to baseball, politics is America's national sport. Since I'm an American, it is no surprise that I often write about politics. Unfortunately, much of what I have had to say is fairly critical about governments and their behaviour: spying, deceiving, torturing and other misdeeds.

(Search) engines of repression

The internet is generally seen as a realm of unrestricted freedom. Since governments have little tolerance for unrestricted freedom, it is hardly shocking that states are increasing their efforts to restrict it.

China, not surprisingly, is leading the way in limiting its citizens' access. All the major search engines, including the allegedly non-evil Google, have bowed to the Chinese government's demand that its citizens' search results be appropriately filtered.[97]

Some companies go above and beyond in the service of oppressive governments. For example, Yahoo turned over a Chinese journalist's emails and this led to him being jailed. Microsoft has routinely blocked anti-government blogs at the behest of China and various other governments.[98]

Western countries also place restrictions on the internet. The United States government is working to protect minors from 'questionable' content and many European governments have laws forbidding or at least limiting Nazi or racist material. Further, the United States government recently requested data about searches from Yahoo and Google, raising concerns about privacy rights. While these situations are much less severe than those of other countries, they still raise concerns about freedom.

There are good reasons to think that governments should restrict information and that companies should cooperate with governments.

First, it is generally accepted that a legitimate function of government is to protect its citizens from harms. Just as this role can involve protecting citizens from physically harmful things such as criminals, terrorists, tainted food and defective products, it can also involve protecting citizens from mentally harmful things such as certain types of images or information. This also gives governments the right to collect information. A company, it can be argued, has no more right to withhold information about political criminals than it has a right to withhold information about murders and rapists.

Second, companies are in the business of making profits and not in the business of undertaking moral crusades for freedom. Just as a car manufacturer must comply with a government's safety laws to sell cars in a country, technical companies must conform to the rules of that country in order to provide services. It is, as various companies are quick to point out, simply the price of doing business. This is not to say that no one should try to defend freedom, but that is not the job of business.

These arguments are reasonable and do provide good grounds for accepting restrictions, information gathering and the cooperation of companies with oppressive governments. However, there are also excellent grounds for taking an alternative view.

First, governments should do more than protect the lives of their citizens – they should also protect the quality of those lives. The possession of basic liberties is an important part of the quality of one's life and privacy and free access to information are, intuitively, basic liberties.

Second, it seems that the citizens whom governments are trying to protect by limiting access to information are the citizens who are in the government. They are no doubt concerned that freedom of information would pose a serious threat to their power and in this they are quite right. From a moral standpoint, it is difficult to argue that those in power have a moral right to protect themselves from the other citizens through secrecy. To claim that they do would be on a par with a Mafia boss claiming that he has a moral right to keep his criminal misdeeds secret because otherwise he would come to harm.

Third, free access to information certainly seems to be far more beneficial to citizens than its restriction. One reason for the success of countries like the United States and Britain is their general openness. Countries that severely restrict information, such as the former Soviet Union, have been shown to fare poorly in comparison.

Fourth, while the business of business is profit, it is absurd to claim that profit serves to justify immoral actions. If profit justified such activities, then we would have to accept that if a company could make money by selling slaves or government secrets, then such practices would be justified. Companies can defend themselves by claiming that accepting such restrictions allows them to set the stage for later openness. That can be a reasonable reply – assuming it is true. Until then, people can rely on software and services designed to allow anonymous searches and surfing.

Closing ranks

An interesting political phenomenon occurred when American and British forces set out to liberate Iraq: people who had opposed the idea of the invasion said that they were now closing ranks behind their leaders and supporting the invasion. Commentators in the American press also endorsed this practice and emphasized the importance of getting behind President Bush and supporting the war. In general, there seemed to be two lines of reasoning behind such views. First, some commentators and citizens made it quite clear that the invasion they had previously regarded as wrong was now something they supported – simply because it was now underway. The second is as follows. It was acceptable to oppose the invasion prior to the actual decision to invade. Once the decision had been reached, citizens were obliged to get behind their leaders and support (or at least not oppose) the invasion.

The first line of reasoning is flawed. If, prior to doing X, doing X is wrong, then it follows that doing X is wrong while X is being done. There does not appear to be any reason to believe that what is wrong becomes right simply in virtue of its being done. If this sort of reasoning were legitimate, there would be no wrong actions – what was wrong would become right in virtue of its implementation. Given that this is absurd, the reasoning must be flawed. Further, this sort of 'reasoning' is not accepted outside of politics. People do not say, for example, that they believed selling tainted food was wrong, but it is acceptable now because they have learned that a company is actually selling tainted food. If there is a difference between these cases and the political situation, then the burden of proof is on those who would claim such a difference. Thus, if the invasion was wrong before it was underway, rolling the troops in did not make it right.

People can, of course, change their moral views and be justified in doing so. But, as has been shown, the mere fact that an action is underway does not justify such a change on any rational ground.

The second line of reasoning has a certain legitimacy. It is an accepted principle that within a democracy the citizens are obligated to follow the decision of the majority. The basis for this principle is found in the work of John Locke. He argues that when an individual consents to be part of the political body, she obligates herself to accept the will of the majority. Without such an obligation, there could be no state – the minority would split away from the majority, destroying the state and returning the people to the state of nature. Since this is undesirable, it is best to preserve the state by going along with the majority.

Given this principle, the citizens who opposed the invasion had a right to express this view and to attempt to get others to agree with them. However, once the decision was made to invade Iraq, the citizens were then obligated to submit graciously to the will of the majority, as they would have expected others to submit had they proven victorious. Thus, once the invasion was underway, the citizens who opposed it would now be obligated to support it.

While this principle is part of what makes the democratic state possible, it must also be noted that throughout history the majority has accepted terrible policies and procedures involving such things as slavery and genocide. It seems intuitively wrong to obligate individuals to support such things simply because the majority has decided in their favour. Thus, it might be tempting to accept that individuals have a right to oppose the decision of the majority.

Before giving into this temptation, it must be noted that majorities have established justice, freedom and equality against the wishes of minorities. The right of women to vote, the end of slavery, and school desegregation were all brought about over the opposition of political minorities. It might be argued that the minorities had no right to oppose such noble purposes. The underlying principle is that when the majority is correct and the minority is wrong, then the minority lacks the right to oppose the majority. The problem is that the majority will almost certainly regard itself as morally correct and as justified in forcing the minority to go along. The principle that the minority can oppose the majority when the majority is in the wrong raises a similar problem – the minority will almost always regard the majority as being wrong – otherwise there would be no disagreement.

While the disagreement creates the problem, it also presents the solution. The minority is obligated to cooperate with the majority to preserve the state but also because the majority could be right. The majority is obligated to allow the minority to oppose the decision because the minority could be in the right. The state, as Socrates would agree, needs its gadfly. Thus, those who opposed the war still have the right to oppose it even after the majority has decided to go to war. In fact, if Socrates is right, they are being good citizens.

Hazing and deterrence

In the United States, hazing is a form of ritualized abuse that occurs as part of the initiation of new members into groups such as fraternities, sororities and sports teams. Hazing varies in intensity from fairly mild rites of passage to situations involving severe mental and physical abuse. While hazing has often been tolerated, the fact that it sometimes results in severe injuries and even fatalities has led to a crackdown on hazing at American colleges and universities.

In January, 2007 two students who attended Florida A&M University, where I teach, were sentenced to two years in prison for their role in a hazing incident. In this incident, one student suffered injuries from being struck repeatedly with canes. The judge noted that although one year would have been a suitable punishment, she decided on two in order to 'send a message'.[99] Presumably she meant that the disproportionate punishment would deter others from hazing.

This situation raises an interesting ethical question: is it morally acceptable to inflict disproportionate punishment in the hope that it will deter others?

From a moral standpoint, the main justifications for punishment have been deterrence, rehabilitation and retribution. If disproportionate punishment serves at least one of these purposes, then it would not be unreasonable to regard it as justifiable. If it does not serve any of these, then it would certainly seem unjustifiable.

It could be claimed that disproportionate punishment is justified because of its deterrent value. One way to argue for this is on utilitarian grounds: while the wrongdoers do suffer excess harm, the inflicted harm is outweighed by the prevented harms. Because future potential crimes are deterred, potential victims will be unharmed and potential criminals will not need to be punished.

One argument against disproportionate punishment is that the threat of legal punishment does not appear to be an effective deterrent. The deterrence value of the law is nicely illustrated by the fact that while the Florida A&M University students were on trial, students from nearby Florida State University were arrested for hazing. Of course, an anecdote, however ironic, does not prove a general point. Fortunately, a general argument can be presented: if the threat of legal punishment had a strong deterrent value, then countries like the United States, which have severe penalties and brutal jails, would have very low crime rates. However, the exact opposite is the case. The fact that American prisons are constantly overcrowded is a stark testament to the ineffectiveness of the threat of legal punishment.

While there is great debate over why the threat of legal punishment is not an effective deterrent, one reason is as follows: If most people rationally weighed such matters as punishment before committing crimes, then the threat of punishment would have deterrent value. However, when most people commit crimes, they are driven by emotional factors such as passions and desires, and hence they do not calculate things rationally. Thus, it is no surprise that the threat of legal punishment has little effect on criminal behaviour.

It could be argued that disproportionate punishment would solve this problem. Proportionate penalties, it could be argued, simply are not frightening enough to have a sufficient emotional impact. But disproportional punishments could be adequately frightening.

In reply, many crimes already have frightening punishments (such as life in prison or death) and these penalties do not seem to deter people effectively. After all, the jails hold many people who are in for life or waiting for their executions. Hence, it seems unlikely that disproportional punishments would have the desired effect.

Moving on to rehabilitation, it seems unlikely that disproportional punishment would have a rehabilitative effect. If a person is punished disproportionately, their reaction would most likely be one of great resentment. If they were to take any lesson away from the experience, it would be that the justice system is unjust. To use an analogy, if a student fails a single quiz and the 'punishment' is that they fail the entire course, this will not teach them to study harder. It will teach them to hate an unfair professor. Thus, disproportionate punishment is not justifiable in terms of rehabilitation.

Finally, there is the matter of retribution. Intuitively, retribution should be proportional to the crime being punished. After all, retribution is generally justified because the wrongdoer deserves to be paid back for her misdeed. Punishing beyond this would go beyond repaying the person for the misdeed – it would be creating another misdeed. Naturally, by definition disproportionate punishment is not punishment proportional to the crime.

Further, retributive punishment is aimed at punishing the wrongdoer for what he did. Inflicting disproportionate punishment to send a message to others is not punishing the wrongdoer for what he did – it is punishing him because of what others might do. This would not

be retribution. Thus, disproportionate punishment cannot be justified on retributive grounds.

Thus, disproportionate punishment is not justified – even when
someone claims that it 'sends a message'.

Forced freedom

In 2003, American-led forces entered the country of Iraq for two
publicly stated reasons. The first was to locate and destroy weapons
of mass destruction. The second was to liberate the Iraqi people from
their own government. While both reasons raise interesting philosophical questions, the focus will be on the second one.

Bush, by stating that the goal of coalition forces is liberation, has
asserted that the coalition is acting on the basis of a moral principle.
While Bush has not and perhaps cannot clearly state this moral principle, it seems to be that democracies have the moral right and even
the duty to bring democracy to people ruled by non-democratic governments.

To make sense of this principle it must first be determined what
makes a government undemocratic and, hence, what makes another
one democratic. Presumably Iraq can be taken as a paradigm case of
an undemocratic state. What makes the Iraqi regime undemocratic
cannot be that it lacks the consent of the people. That the regime has
the general consent of the people is shown by two facts: large
numbers of people continued to fight in its defence and the majority
of Iraqis did not rise against the government despite opportunities to
do so.

It also cannot be that the regime is repressive and mistreats minorities, though it is guilty on both counts. America has a long history of
repression and the mistreatment of minorities, such as slavery, is as
American as apple pie. The UK also has a similar history – just ask the
Irish, for example. Yet both are considered legitimate democracies.

What other than political rhetoric marks Iraq as an undemocratic
regime? The most plausible answer seems to be that the regime did

not permit truly free elections and the people were denied proper participation in the government.

Thus, a democratic government must permit free elections and the people must have proper participation in government.

Now the main question can be addressed: is the moral principle presented above justified? The answer depends on the basis of political legitimacy.

Thinkers such as John Locke argue that given natural equality and natural rights, only a democratic form of government is justified. Governments that violate these rights are tyrannies and, as such, are illegitimate and should be resisted. Such governments are, in effect, criminals who are robbing the citizens of their legitimate rights. Given that it is at least morally acceptable to aid a person who is being robbed of her money by an individual, it would seem to follow that it is also at least morally acceptable to aid people who are being robbed of their rights by a state.

It can be argued further that democratic states have an obligation to bring democracy to others. If one person accepts the principle that people have the right to be left in peace and he sees another person being attacked, it would seem that he has an obligation to help that other person. This is because that in accepting a principle one also accepts the obligation to act upon it. If a person asserts that he can accept a principle yet not be obligated to act upon it, he is acting like a person who claims to accept a speed limit yet also claims she has no reason to drive in accord with that limit. In both cases the person clearly fails to grasp what it means to accept a principle or law.

Turning to the matter of democracy, if citizens of a democratic state are aware that another state is not democratic, then they are under an obligation to bring democracy to that state. As citizens of a democracy, they accept the principle that people have certain rights and that non-democratic states violate these rights. If the citizens do not act upon their principle, then they are rejecting it – thus rejecting democracy itself. Thus, people that wish to remain committed to democracy are obligated to bring democracy to others.

Thus, if the coalition democracies are truly in Iraq to bring democracy to the people, they are acting in a morally correct manner. Of course, one problem with principles is that they are not to be applied only when they are convenient. If the coalition has an obligation to liberate the people of Iraq, then they have an obligation to liberate all people who live under non-democratic governments – even those people who do not happen to live over vast supplies of oil. Thus, if action had to be taken against Iraq, then it would seem that action must be taken against countries like Cuba, Korea and China. Further, action would need to be taken against countries like Saudi Arabia and other oil sheikdoms – while they tend to be allied with the democracies, they are obviously not democracies and, hence, must be liberated. Given the fiasco that was the 2000 US presidential election, perhaps the US needs to be liberated as well.

John Locke and cyber-vigilantism

The development of peer-to-peer networks has allowed internet users to swap files with each other in an easy and convenient manner. As should come as no surprise, a fair number of the swapped files (typically music and movie files) are being exchanged in violation of copyright laws. Unlike the famous Napster case, there is no main organization for law enforcement officials to target – only a multitude of users linked in networks.

In response to this situation, a member of the United States Congress, Howard Berman, proposed a bill[100] that will allow copyright holders to attack, via computer hacking, computers owned by those who violate (or allegedly violate) such copyrights. Such attacks could involve infecting the copyrighted files with viruses designed to make them useless or inserting programs to track the use of files to make sure the copyright is not violated. There are, of course, some restrictions – the US Department of Justice must be notified of such an attack, the attacks must be limited to those engaged in copyright violations and must cause no more than $50 (US) in damage. While this proposed law seems to be clearly intended to benefit the major players in the entertainment industry, it would open the hacking door to anyone who holds a copyright.

While this proposed law and others like it might seem to be purely within the realm of law, they are philosophically interesting. While John Locke was obliviously not aware of peer-to-peer networks, his philosophical views can be applied to this situation. As Locke[101] notes, when people leave the state of nature and enter into political society, they give up their right to punish others and seek retribution. This right is transferred to the state which is to act on behalf of its citizens. This view prevails in the United States and most countries – citizens are not allowed, in general, to take the law into their own hands. Instead, the state's law enforcement and judicial components handle such matters. However, Locke notes that when authority is lacking, people are in the state of nature. In this state of nature people are permitted to judge their own cases and seek retribution against those who have done them wrong. This is, of course, because they have no higher authority to which they can appeal. Locke does not, of course, endorse uncontrolled vengeance: he holds that retribution must be proportional to damage suffered and within the limits of reason and conscience.

Given that computer networks span the globe and the obvious lack of a world government (or even a truly effective international legal system), it seems evident that copyright holders and those who violate those copyrights will often be in the state of nature. As an example, US copyright holders might have their copyrights violated by people living in countries that do not recognize American legal authority or even by people who live in areas of the world that lack a centralized authority. In such cases, it would be all but impossible to bring about effective legal action against the offenders. However, being connected to the internet, the offenders are accessible to hacking. Such attacks would be practical and, more important from the philosopher's standpoint, ethical as well – provided that the attack was limited to rendering the stolen property useless. After all, the damage would be proportional to the harm and it is a well-established moral principle that a thief is not wronged when the rightful owner reclaims her property.

One obvious objection is that attacks could not be justified if launched against citizens in countries that permit legal redress in such cases. In response, it can be argued that even in such cases the state of nature still exists. The internet, even within the confines of a single country, has been aptly described as a digital 'wild west' with no sheriff in town. Hence, such attacks would still be justified.

Of course, as proponents of such laws should note, the moral sword cuts both ways. If copyright holders have the right to attack those who violate their copyrights, it would follow that similar attacks would be justified as well. The general principle behind the proposed law is that people have a right to protect what belongs to them and hacking is a legitimate means of achieving that end, provided that the relevant authorities are unable or unwilling to take action in such situations. Thus, for example, it would seem that people would have a moral and legal right to hack into computers that contain information about them that was gathered improperly, provided that the government failed to act to protect their privacy. As a specific example, if a company secretly gathered information about a person's web surfing habits, that person would have the right to hack that company's computers to render that information useless. The same principle would also seem to extend that right to include attacks by individuals on governments. It also seems reasonable to extend the principle further so that it legitimizes additional types of hacking that are aimed at righting wrongs, but such considerations are beyond the scope of this work.

Terror and torture

The terrible threats presented by terrorism have led to a serious reconsideration of torture as a means of extracting information. While there is considerable debate regarding the legality of torture, this provocation is focused on the morality of torture in the context of the fight against terror.

While most people regard torture as evil, there are reasonable moral arguments in its favour. The most common argument is a utilitarian one: the harm prevented by gathering information by torture can outweigh the moral harms inflicted by the practice of torture.

A favourite example used by torture proponents, such as Harvard's Alan Dershowitz,[102] is the 1995 case of Abdul Hakim Murad. After being tortured for over a month by Philippine police, Murad revealed various terrorist plans, including a plot to kill the Pope. Because of cases like this, one might conclude that the evil of torture can be outweighed by its good consequences – such as preventing murder.

If the evil of using torture is outweighed by its potential good consequences, then the matter of its effectiveness needs to be resolved. If torture is not an effective means of gaining reliable information, then there will be no good consequences to outweigh the evil of engaging in torture. If this is the case, then torture cannot be justified in this manner.

While there is significant debate over the general effectiveness of torture, it appears that it is not a particularly effective means of acquiring accurate information.

First, consider the American and European witch trials. During these trials, a significant number of people confessed, under brutal torture, to being witches. If torture is an effective means of acquiring truthful information, then these trials provided reasonable evidence for the existence of witches, magic, the Devil and, presumably, God. However, it seems rather odd that such metaphysical matters could be settled by the application of the rack, the iron maiden and the thumb screw. As such, the effectiveness of torture is rather questionable.

Second, extensive studies of torture[103] show that it is largely ineffective as a means of gathering correct information.[104] For example, the Gestapo's use of torture against the French resistance in the 1940s and the French use of torture against the Algerian resistance in the 1950s both proved largely ineffective. As another example, Diederik Lohman, a senior researcher for Human Rights Watch, found that the torture of suspected criminals typically yields information that is not accurate. A final and rather famous example is that of Ibn al-Shaykh al-Libi. Under torture, al-Libi claimed that Al Qaeda had significant links to Iraq. However, as he himself later admitted, there were no such links. Thus, the historical record seems to count against the effectiveness of torture.

Third, as history and basic human psychology show, most people will say almost anything to end terrible suffering. For example, a former prisoner from Abu Ghraib told the *New York Times* that, after being tortured, he confessed to being Osama Bin Laden to put an end to his mistreatment. Similar things occur in the context of domestic law enforcement in the United States: suspects subjected to threats and mistreatments have confessed to crimes they did not commit. As such, torture seems to be a rather dubious way of acquiring reliable intelligence.

Given that torture is not effective as a means of gathering reliable information, the utilitarian argument in its favour must be rejected. This is because torturing people is not likely to yield any good consequences.

Despite its ineffectiveness as a means of extracting information directly, torture does seem to be an effective means towards another end, namely that of intimidation. History has shown that authoritarian societies successfully employed torture as a means of political control and as a means of creating informers. Ironically, while actual torture rarely yields reliable information, the culture of fear created by the threat of torture often motivates people to bring information to those in power.

Given its effectiveness as a tool of coercion and intimidation, torture and the threat of torture could be used as weapons against terror. If the threat of torture is both credible and terrible enough, then the likelihood of terrorist activity could be reduced and the number of useful informants could increase significantly.

From a moral standpoint, if torture were to prove effective as a means of reducing terrorist activity, then it could be argued that the use of torture is morally acceptable. The gist of the argument is that the moral harms of threatening and utilizing torture are outweighed by the moral consequences – namely a reduction in terrorist activity.

While this argument has a certain appeal, it faces three problems. First, it seems likely that adopting torture and the threat of torture as weapons would be morally harmful to the society in question. To see that this is likely, one needs to merely consider the nature of societies that have already embraced the use of torture. Second, the use of torture as a means of coercion and intimidation certainly seems to be a form of terrorism. As such, the reduction in one type of terrorism would be, ironically, offset by the increase in another. Third, terrorism is denounced as a moral evil and its alleged opponents, such as George Bush, seem to revel in claiming the moral high ground. However, a society that accepts the use of torture cannot claim the moral high ground – they are walking the same ground as the terrorists. Thus, it would seem that the use of torture is not morally acceptable.

Mining your business

While security agencies such as the National Security Agency prefer secrecy, their actions do make the headlines. For example, *USA Today* revealed that the NSA had created a database of billions of calls made within the United States. There is also evidence that the NSA has been engaged in other forms of domestic spying.

These revelations raise the classic debate between privacy and security. From a moral standpoint, these practices could be justified on a utilitarian basis: if the benefits to security outweigh the harms of privacy violations, then they could be regarded as morally acceptable. The NSA takes this position – they claim that if they were able to prevent another 9/11, the privacy violations would be justified.

The NSA claims that its database has helped foil terrorist plots. If so, perhaps their actions are justified. Unfortunately, the NSA refuses to provide any details that could be used to confirm these alleged successes. So, whether their actions are justified or not remains a secret. However, it is possible to continue the discussion using what is known.

The US has claimed success by capturing Iyman Faris. He allegedly plotted to destroy the Brooklyn Bridge using a blowtorch. However, he was not located via domestic spying – he was identified by a captured Qaeda leader. This indicates the government is willing to publicize its successes and implies the NSA has not succeeded despite its privacy violations. Thus, the utilitarian justification for their actions seems groundless – at least until evidence of their success is available.

Of course, there are good grounds to doubt the NSA's chances of success. Interestingly enough, the NSA was able to tap the phone lines of a Qaeda safe house and learn of a Qaeda meeting attended by two of the 9/11 hijackers. However, bureaucratic slowness and jealousy resulted in a slow turnover of the data and the attack was obviously not thwarted. This suggests that even if the NSA is able to acquire data, it might not be able to use it. Thus, until the NSA can demonstrate an ability to use the data, there seems to be little reason to believe that their actions are morally acceptable. They seem to be violating people's privacy and yielding nothing in return.

Another reason to doubt the NSA's chances of success is the ease with which its methods can be thwarted. First, terrorists can easily acquire communication technology that would keep their communications out of the database. Second, terrorists can and do rely on methods of communication that do not involve phones or even electronics at all. Given these methods of avoidance, it is unlikely that the NSA database will contain terrorist communications. Instead, they have probably only violated the privacy of millions of people.

But, suppose the above argument is mistaken – imagine terrorist communications are logged within the database. One problem is locating these terrorist communications among the billions of calls. The proposed solution, data mining, has proven effective in the world of business. The basic idea is that the data is examined for meaningful patterns. In the case of business, this might involve establishing a credit card customer's buying patterns so that misuses of her account can be spotted. In the case of security, this might involve finding patterns connecting people with a known terrorist, thus identifying a potential terrorist cell.

Effective data mining on the scale envisioned by the NSA that could sort out terrorist from non-terrorist patterns would require an extensive software and hardware system. Such as system, Trailblazer, was supposed to enable the NSA to do this. Instead, it failed miserably at the price of almost one billion dollars. From a utilitarian standpoint, the billion dollars wasted on Trailblazer could have been more effectively used in ways that did not violate privacy. As such, the NSA's activities do not seem to be morally justified.

Finally, suppose that Trailblazer could be made operational. Even in this hypothetical paradise there is still a serious problem, namely that of false positives. Since terrorists do have interactions with non-terrorists, these non-terrorists could very well end up in the patterns identified by data mining software. Given the zeal with which the United States has illegally detained people, there would be a real possibility that innocent people would be detained and perhaps even tortured. For the NSA to be morally justified in using such data mining, it would have to be the case that the benefits gained from this practice would outweigh the possibility of doing great harm to the innocent. This seems unlikely.

Patriot games

The recent war in Iraq, revelations of presidential dishonesty and the ongoing battle against terrorism have once again brought the topic of patriotism into the public consciousness. In democratic countries like the United States and Great Britain, the nature of patriotism has been a matter of great controversy. Fortunately for the confused masses, Britney Spears provided CNN with her views on patriotism: 'I think we should just trust the president in every decision he makes and we should just support that, and be faithful in what happens.'[105]

While Ms Spears is not generally regarded as a profound thinker, her view of patriotism has a certain merit. If patriotism is taken to be a love of and dedication to one's country, then this love and dedication would seem to obligate the patriotic citizens of a democracy to trust and support the leaders they elected. After all, even a liberal thinker like John Locke[106] argued that citizens are obligated to go along with the decision of the majority, even if they disagree with that decision. On practical grounds, dissent and disobedience could prove harmful to a country, especially in troubled times when a unified effort is needed. Thus, it might be concluded that Ms Spears' view of patriotism is correct and good citizens should fall behind their leaders like obedient sheep.

However, this is not the case. A fairly neutral view of patriotism, and hence a proper starting point, is that it is the love of and dedication to one's country. Using this definition as a starting point, two arguments will be presented to show that being truly patriotic in a democratic country does not mean giving the leaders the degree of trust and obedience that Ms Spears endorses.

First, there is the matter of the nature of country. It seems reasonable to accept that a country is not simply the land, government or people – it also refers to the ideals of the nation. While a fascist state would hold such unquestioning trust and complete obedience as ideals, this is not the case in democracies like the United States and Great Britain. The right to dissent and the right to be sceptical of leaders are part of the ideals of such democracies. After all, a key foundation of the modern democracy is the individuality and independence of each citizen as well as her freedom of thought and expression. The notion that citizens should simply believe and obey goes against these ideals; hence the proper patriotism in such democracies cannot be the sort of patriotism Ms Spears had in mind.

Second, there is the matter of love and dedication. While there are a variety of philosophies of love, it is generally accepted that if a person truly loves something, then she wants what is best for it or at the very least desires that it should not be harmed. This view of love is supported by the fact that it would be rather odd for someone to claim they loved something, yet also claim that they wished the thing ill. In terms of dedication, one who is dedicated to his country would act upon this love and hence attempt to bring about what is good and prevent what is bad for his country.

What remains to be determined is whether the sort of trust and support advocated by Ms Spears is good for the United States (or any country).

History shows that terrible things tend to happen when citizens choose to provide (or are coerced into providing) such unquestioning support. While the examples of Hitler and Stalin are certainly overused, they provide two clear cases of the all-too-common results of such unquestioning obedience: ruined nations and multitudes of corpses. Unless ruin and death are good, it seems clear that such unquestioning support is not consistent with the love of one's country.

An objection is that rulers like Hitler, Stalin and other such dictators are exceptional cases and, of course, democratic rulers would certainly never do such terrible things. Thus, obedience would be consistent with patriotism.

While this objection is certainly reasonable, history has shown that even democratic rulers are prone to lying and supporting harmful, evil activities. Looking back, for example, at American history, one can see democratic rulers lying about important matters and, far worse, supporting such things as slavery, racial segregation and wars of conquest. Obviously, slavery alone did terrible harm to America and her people.

In light of these facts, one must accept that trusting and obeying even a democratic ruler without question would be a terrible risk. While the leader might act well, it seems more likely that he would also act badly – even more so if he knew he would not be questioned.

Thus, to be a patriot is not to give unthinking support to one's leader. The true patriot should always ask 'is this leader doing what is best for the country?' If she is, then the patriot should lend his support. If not, the patriot should be prepared to defend his country against this enemy.

Terror and medicine

There are many ways to die and limited resources available to fight these ways. Hence, one important moral problem is deciding how these limited resources should be allocated.

In matters involving strangers, people tend to take a utilitarian approach. To be specific, most people will accept, on the basis of their moral intuitions, that the distribution of resources that prevents the most deaths is the distribution that should be chosen. This intuition is easily tested: Imagine that a fast-acting disease is ravaging two remote towns. Only one plane is available and it can reach only one town in time. One town has 10,000 inhabitants, the other 1,000. Intuitively, the plane should fly to the larger town to save more lives.

The intuitions that worked well within the confines of a philosophical problem seem to fail in the actual world – the relevant resources do not seem to be distributed to prevent the most deaths. This discrepancy raises many questions of philosophical interest. However, to make the discussion manageable and concrete, I will focus on medical neglect and terrorism.

To date, vast resources have been committed to the war on terror. Given this massive and ongoing expenditure, a rational person would expect two things. First, that terrorism is a threat in proportion to the resources expended. Second, that the expenditure has yielded proportional results. If the resources expended are not proportional to the threat or are not yielding proportional results, then it would make sense to use the resources in other ways to prevent more deaths.

In regards to the first, terrorism does not seem to be a threat in proportion to the resources expended. A way to measure a deadly threat is by determining the number of deaths per year – the more deaths, the greater the threat. For the United States the worst year was 2001 – about 3,000 people were murdered on September 11.

Those deaths were horrific, but the Institute of Medicine estimates that about 18,000 Americans die every year from a lack of healthcare coverage.[107] That is the equivalent of six September 11s every year. One would think that given the vast number of deaths, America would mobilize to fight a war on the lack of healthcare. If billions should be spent to prevent another September 11, even more should be spent to prevent the equivalent of six. Unfortunately, this does not seem to be the case.

Of course, terrorism is an international problem. Perhaps if the death toll includes all relevant deaths, the vast expenditure can be morally justified. However, this is not the case. While many people are brutally murdered by terrorists around the world, the number of people dying from medical neglect is truly staggering. For example, it is estimated that visceral leishmaniasis (better known as kala azar), a parasitic infection, afflicts half a million people a year and kills at least 200,000. It costs a mere $200 (US) to cure a person, but this disease is largely neglected by Western governments.[108] Of course, kala azar is but one disease among many. Given just these numbers, it would seem from a moral standpoint that more resources should be expended on addressing medical neglect, even if that means diverting resources from the war on terror.

It can be objected that the comparison is unfair – it focuses on the number of people killed by terrorists and not the deaths prevented by fighting terrorism. To use an analogy, it would be foolish to say that the resources spent on preventing a disease were poorly spent because now there are few cases – the point of prevention is to have as few cases as possible. This leads to the second concern, namely that of results.

If the war on terror has proportional results, then it would be morally acceptable to expend the resources in question. To be honest, it can be rather hard to show that something is the cause of something else not happening. However, there seems to be little trustworthy evidence that the resources expended in the war on terror are preventing anything close to the number of deaths that would be prevented by using even a fraction of those resources to counter medical neglect. This is not to say that resources should not be expended to deal with terrorism, but that it is right to expend resources in ways that will prevent so many more deaths.

Appearance

In Plato's *Republic*[109] Glaucon presents a challenge between the perfectly unjust man and the perfectly just man. The unjust man is truly unjust but has the skills and resources he needs for a prosperous life and to get away with his misdeeds while maintaining a reputation for justice. The perfectly just man is the exact opposite – he has nothing but his justice and a false reputation for being unjust. The challenge given to Socrates is to prove that the life of the just man is preferable even under the stated conditions.

On the face of it, the unjust life seems preferable. The unjust person reaps the benefits of a good reputation while avoiding actually having to do good deeds. Further, he is free to use all the tools of injustice to get what he wants. He has all this because, by hypothesis, he cannot be exposed. While members of the Bush administration seem to want to be perfectly unjust men, they are not quite up to the task of maintaining the façade of justice – despite strenuous efforts to do so.

A short while ago it was revealed that the Bush administration was paying members of the press to put a positive light on the administration. It has also been revealed that the Rendon Group had been given a government contract to set the stage for Hussein's removal. This process allegedly including reporters like Judith Miller to bogus WMD sources. More recently it was revealed that the Pentagon was employing American soldiers to write positive articles about Iraq. Contractors translated the articles into Arabic and bribed the Iraqi press to print them as news. This process was implemented by one of the three contractors who were given $300 million to create ideas for managing the international perception of the United States. In short, the United States was attempting to create the illusion of justice and was caught in the process.[110] In retrospect, the United States should not have done this. There is a very practical reason why this is the case.

The practical reason involves cost. One reason not to do good deeds is that they involve expending resources to aid others that could be used for self-benefit. For example, rather than spending money to help disaster victims, a person could buy herself a new pair of shoes or an Xbox 360. One reason to do bad deeds is that such deeds are seen as yielding more profit than good deeds. For example, a company can make more profits by underpaying workers and not paying its fair share of taxes.

In the case of buying a good reputation, resources are being expended in order to create the illusion of goodness. But, of course, a good reputation can also be acquired by expending resources to actually do good deeds. For example, the money spent on bribing the press and hiring contractors could have been used to build schools, treat sick children, or any number of good things.

Obviously, from a moral standpoint, it is better actually to do the good deeds and not worry about the reputation. However, from a purely pragmatic standpoint, the main issue focuses on the question of which approach has the best chance of creating the greatest reputation boost.

While specific cases will vary, it seems reasonable to believe that if the same amount of resources is expended, then actually doing good deeds will yield the best chance of creating the greatest reputation boost. This is because one is likely to get caught trying to create the illusion of goodness and this will create the opposite of the intended effect. Instead of looking virtuous, the country will be exposed as deceitful and manipulative. These are not exactly the qualities one would ascribe to a just nation.

By actually doing good deeds, there is little chance of such a negative effect occurring. There is, of course, the risk that good deeds will be misinterpreted. However, attempts to create the illusion of goodness are more likely to backfire than attempts to actually do good. Thus, if resources are going to be expended to boost a country's reputation, then there are excellent pragmatic and moral reasons to use these resources to actually do good deeds.

Conclusion

I hope you enjoyed this book and found the contents thought-provoking and that your interest in philosophy has increased. At this point, you might be wondering if there is a mission or agenda behind this book. There is.

While many books aim at encouraging the reader to accept a certain set of alleged truths, my mission was quite different.

Philosophy, as I see it, is not about believing certain tenets or accepting certain dogmas. Philosophy is about asking questions, seeking answers and entertaining doubt. Critical to that endeavour is a willingness to be rationally provoked by different ideas and to see where they might lead – assuming they turn out to be worth following. This is not to say that we must be endlessly locked in questions and doubt. Most of the time, life requires us to take a definite stand and to act upon our convictions. At that point we should choose what we see as the very best belief. Naturally, we should temper the strength of our belief and the nature of our actions with the knowledge that we could be mistaken. After all, a little doubt goes a long way in avoiding trouble.

Given this view, which is not shared by everyone, my hope is that this book has provoked you into considering issues in a new light so that you can critically evaluate your own views on the matters discussed. If you find that you disagree with me, so much the better. The search for truth and wisdom benefits most from dissent. It is uncritical agreement that derails this search and leaves people stuck in the dark. Of course, if you do agree with me on some points, that is cool, too.

Thanks for reading this book. Since the world shows no signs that it will stop provoking me, you can expect to see philosophical provocations continue in print and online. Naturally, when I find the Truth, my work will be done and I can stop writing. But I do not see that happening anytime soon.

Notes

1. Kant discusses the metaphysical self in I. Kant (1977), *Prolegomena to Any Future Metaphysics* (trans. P. Carus, rev. with intro by James Ellington). Indianapolis, IN: Hackett Publishers.

2. P. Bloom (2004), *Descartes' Baby: How The Science Of Child Development Explains What Makes Us Human.* New York: Basic Books.

3. Rifkin's concerns are duly noted in J. Kluger (1997), 'Will We Follow the Sheep?' *Time*, http://www.time.com/time/magazine/article/ 0,9171, 986024-2,00.html.

4. The distinction between the cats is discussed in K. Hays (2003), 'Cloned Cat isn't a Carbon Copy', CBS News, http://www.cbsnews.com/stories/ 2003/01/21/tech/main537380.shtml.

5. Descartes' primary discussion of the mind occurs in his second and sixth meditations. See R. Descartes (1988), *The Philosophical Writings of Descartes: Volume 1* (trans. J. Cottingham, R. Stoothoff and D. Murdoch). Avon: Cambridge University Press.

6. Locke discusses the nature of the mind in Book II, Chapter XXVII of his *An Essay Concerning Human Understanding.* See J. Locke (1975), *An Essay Concerning Human Understanding* (ed. P. Nidditch). Oxford: Oxford University Press.

7. Hume presents his bundle theory of the mind in Book I, Section VI of his *Treatise.* See D. Hume (1989), *A Treatise of Human Nature* (2nd edn) (ed. P. Nidditch). Oxford: Oxford University Press.

8. The *Phaedo* is Plato's dialogue about the soul and the possibility of continued existence after the death of the body. See Plato (1981), *Five Dialogues: Euthyphro, Apology, Crito, Meno, Phaedo* (trans. G. Grube). Indianapolis, IN: Hacket Publishing Company, Inc.

9. Descartes' presentation of mind–body dualism occurs primarily in his second and sixth meditations. See R. Descartes (1988), *The Philosophical Writings of Descartes: Volume II* (trans. J. Cottingham, R. Stoothoff and D. Murdoch). Avon: Cambridge University Press. He also discusses the mind in his 'Comments on a Certain Broadsheet'. See R. Descartes (1988), *The Philosophical Writings of Descartes: Volume I*

(trans. J. Cottingham, R. Stoothoff and D. Murdoch). Avon: Cambridge University Press.

10. J. Moseley, K. O'Malley, N. Petersen, T. Menke, B. Brody, D. Kuykendall, J. Hollingsworth, C. Ashton and N. Wray (2002), 'A Controlled Trial of Arthroscopic Surgery for Osteoarthritis of the Knee'. *The New England Journal of Medicine*, http://content.nejm.org/cgi/content/abstract/347/2/81.

11. S. Graham (2001), 'Parkinson's Patients Feel the Placebo Effect'. *Scientific America*, http://www.sciam.com/article.cfm?articleID= 000A97F89525-1C60-B882809EC588ED9F.

12. This is discussed in S. Graham(2004), 'Scientists See How Placebo Effect Eases Pain'. *Scientific America*, http://www.sciam.com/article.cfm? article ID=000B6140-F61E-1034-B61E83414B7F0000&sc=I100322.

13. Extensive details of this virtual reality treatment are provided in H. Hoffman (2004), 'Virtual Reality Therapy'. *Scientific America*, August, 58–65.

14. The results of this study are concisely presented in B. Carey (2006), 'A Shocker: Partisan Thought is Unconscious'. *New York Times*, http://www. nytimes.com/2006/01/24/science/24find.html?ex=1177819200&en= 7f01162b58b02786&ei=5070.

15. C. Hanley (2006), 'Poll: Half of America Still Believes in WMD'. *Bangor Daily News*, 7 August, A5.

16. C. Hanley (2006), 'Poll: Half of America Still Believes in WMD'. *Bangor Daily News*, 7 August, A5.

17. Yes, this group really exists. Their website location is http://www.godhatesfags.com/main/index.html.

18. J. Rennie (2002), '15 Answers to Creationist Nonsense'. *Scientific America*, July, 78–85.

19. 'Occam' is sometimes spelled 'Ockham', thus creating some confusion. An excellent source for Occam's writings is Occam (1957), *Philosophical Writings* (ed. and trans. P. Boehner). Edinburgh: Nelson.

20. Aristotle makes a case for the First Mover in his *Physics*. See Aristotle (1991), *The Complete Works of Aristotle* (two vols) (ed. J. Barnes). Princeton: Princeton University Press.

21. Descartes' presentation of dualism occurs primarily in his second and

sixth meditations. See R. Descartes (1988), *The Philosophical Writings of Descartes: Volume II* (trans. J. Cottingham, R. Stoothoff and D. Murdoch). Avon: Cambridge University Press.

22. J. Alter (2005), 'Monkey See, Monkey Do'. *Newsweek*, 15 August, 27.
23. Ibid.
24. Extensive information about this institute and the views of its members can be found at http://www.discovery.org/.
25. J. Alter (2005), 'Monkey See, Monkey Do'. *Newsweek*, 15 August, 27.
26. B. Flam (2006), 'One Big STEP: Another Major Study Confirms that Distant Prayers Do Not Heal the Sick'. *Skeptical Inquirer*, July/August 2006, 5–6.
27. Ibid.
28. Ibid.
29. Socrates', famous claim that he knew only that he knew nothing occurs in the *Apology*. See Plato (1896), *The Dialogues of Plato* (3rd edn) (trans. B. Jowett). Oxford: Oxford University Press.
30. His sceptical method is presented at length in his first meditation. See R. Descartes (1988), *The Philosophical Writings of Descartes: Volume II* (trans. J. Cottingham, R. Stoothoff and D. Murdoch). Avon: Cambridge University Press.
31. Plato's theory of love is presented in the *Symposium*. See Plato (1896), *The Dialogues of Plato* (3rd edn) (trans. B. Jowett). Oxford: Oxford University Press.
32. Kant presents this distinction in I. Kant (1965), *Critique of Pure Reason* (trans. J. Ellington). New York: St Martin's Press.
33. D. Armstrong (1989), *Universals*, Westview, CO: Boulder.
34. K. Campbell (1990), *Abstract Particulars*. Cambridge: Basil Blackwell.
35. Hume discussed cause and effect in Part III of Book I of his *Treatise*. See D. Hume (1989), *A Treatise of Human Nature* (2nd edn) (ed. P. Nidditch). Oxford: Oxford University Press.
36. Her book is R. Byrne (2006), *The Secret*. New York: Beyond Words Publishing. There is also a DVD of the same name, published by Prime Time Video that reveals the secret in a multimedia format.
37. J. Adler (2007), 'Decoding 'The Secret''. *Newsweek*, http://www.msnbc.msn.com/id/17314883/site/newsweek/.

38. The official website of *The Secret*, http://thesecret.tv/ provides extensive information about the book and the film.

39. The text of this law is conveniently provided by the United States Department of Labor at http://www.dol.gov/oasam/regs/statutes/titleix.htm.

40. This is discussed in D. Blume (1993), 'Getting Tough on College Sports'. *Chronicle of Higher Education*, http://chronicle.com/che-data/articles.dir/articles-40.dir/issue-04.dir/04a03901.htm.

41. The general inequality continues as discussed in T. Lewin (2006), 'At Colleges, Women are Leaving Men in the Dust'. *The New York Times*, http://www.nytimes.com/2006/07/09/education/09college.html?ex=1310097600&en=cd9efba2e9595dec&ei=5088&partner=rssnyt&emc=rss.

42. J. Gavora (2002), *Tilting the Playing Field*. San Francisco, CA: Encounter Books.

43. C. Sommers (2000), *The War against Boys – How Misguided Feminism is Harming our Young Men*. New York: Simon & Shuster.

44. This phenomenon is discussed in J. Scelfo (2005), 'Bad Girls Go Wild'. *Newsweek*, 13 June, 66–7.

45. For those not familiar with Baskin Robbins, they are legendary for the number of ice cream flavours they offer. See http://www.baskinrobbins.com/.

46. L. Brizendine (2006), *The Female Brain* (1st edn). New York: Morgan Road Books.

47. J. Scelfo and P. Tyre, 'Why Girls Will Be Girls'. *Newsweek*, 31 July, 46–7.

48. These statistics are presented in P. Tyre (2005), 'Boy Brains, Girl Brains'. *Newsweek*, 19 September, 59.

49. J. Scelfo and P. Tyre, 'Why Girls Will Be Girls'. *Newsweek*, 31 July, 46–7.

50. Plato (1979), *The Republic* (trans. R. Larson). Arlington Heights, IL: Harlan Davidson.

51. P. Tyre (2005), 'Boy Brains, Girl Brains'. *Newsweek*, 19 September, 59.

52. This practice was initially discussed in J. Borland (2002), 'ISP Download Caps to Slow Swapping?'. *News.com*, http://news.com.com/2100-1023-975320.html.

53. An excellent summary of the various attempts to censor video games is

presented in M. Irwin (2006), 'Rated V for Violence'. *PC Magazine*, 7 March, 152–3.

54. Plato's argument is presented in Book X of his *Republic*. See Plato (1941), *The Republic of Plato* (trans. F. Cornford). London: Oxford University Press.

55. Aristotle's discussion of vice and virtue occurs in his *Nichomachean Ethics*. See Aristotle (1991), *The Complete Works of Aristotle* (two vols) (ed. J. Barnes). Princeton, NJ: Princeton University Press.

56. K. Springen (2006), 'This is Your Brain on Alien Killer Pimps of Nazi Doom'. *Newsweek*, 11 December, 48.

57. For the latest on his work see S. Handelman (2007), 'The Memory Hacker'. *Popular Science*, 27 April, 66.

58. According to the BBC (2003) even Prince Charles is worried about the 'grey goo'. See http://news.bbc.co.uk/2/hi/science/nature/2982133.stm.

59. I made this up, but rather like it. In fact, I encourage everyone to use it.

60. *Medical News Today* reported the first clinical trial in this area in 2006. See http://www.medicalnewstoday.com/medicalnews.php?newsid=40669.

61. See M. Darnovsky (2004), 'Revisiting Sex Selection: The Growing Popularity of New Sex Selection Methods Revives an Old Debate'. *Council for Responsible Genetics*, http://www.gene-watch.org/gene-watch/articles/17-1darnovsky.html.

62. Mr. Schmeiser's ongoing battle is documented at http://www.percyschmeiser.com/. CBC News has also covered this story at http://www. cbc.ca/news/background/genetics_modification/ percyschmeiser.html.

63. J. Ackerman (2002), 'Food: How Safe?'. *National Geographic*, May, 2–50.

64. Nexia's site is http://www.nexiabiotech.com/en/00_home/index.php.

65. S. Newman (2001), 'Australian Mouse Study Confirms CRG Warning', http://www.gene-watch.org/genewatch/articles/14-2mousestuart.html.

66. Vehicle death tolls for the United States are updated at the National Highway Traffic Safety Administration at http://www.nhtsa.dot.gov/.

67. J. Mosley, K. O'Malley, N. Petersen, T. Menke, B. Brody, D. Kuykendall, J. Hollingsworth, C. Ashton and N. Wray (2002), 'A Controlled Trial of

Arthroscopic Surgery for Osteoarthritis of the Knee'. *The New England Journal of Medicine*, http://content.nejm.org/cgi/content/abstract/347/2/81.

68. The book itself is J. Frey (2003), *A Million Little Pieces*. New York: Random House. The lies were discussed in M. Peyser (2006), 'The Ugly Truth'. *Newsweek*, 23 January, 62–4.

69. The noble lie is presented in Book III of the *Republic*. See Plato (1979), *The Republic* (trans. R. Larson). Arlington Heights, IL: Harlan Davidson.

70. M. Peyser (2006), 'The Ugly Truth'. *Newsweek*, 23 January, 62.

71. Ibid.

72. Fox News reported this at http://www.foxnews.com/story/0,2933,230838,00.html.

73. The book itself is R. Byrne (2006), *The Secret*. New York: Beyond Words Publishing. The work is discussed in J. Adler (2007), 'Decoding "The Secret"'. *Newsweek*, http://www.msnbc.msn.com/id/17314883/site/newsweek.

74. J. Adler (2007), 'Decoding "The Secret"'. *Newsweek*, http://www.msnbc.msn.com/id/17314883/site/newsweek.

75. J. Adler and T. Weingarten (2005), 'The Flap over Foie Gras'. *Newsweek*, 2 May, 58.

76. Ibid.

77. Ibid.

78. Ibid.

79. Plato's argument for censorship is presented in Book X of the *Republic*. See Plato (1941), *The Republic of Plato* (trans. F. Cornford). London: Oxford University Press.

80. See the *Poetics* in Aristotle (1991), *The Complete Works of Aristotle* (two vols) (ed. J. Barnes). Princeton, NJ: Princeton University Press.

81. See G. Edgers (2003), 'Sculptor Sues Fidelity to Keep his Artistic Vision Intact'. *Boston Globe*, http://www.boston.com/ae/theater_arts/articles/2003/10/07/sculptor_sues_fidelity_to_keep_his_artistic_vision_intact/.

82. H. Hansmann and M. Santilli (1997), 'Authors' and Artists' Moral Rights: A Comparative Legal and Economic Analysis'. *The Journal of Legal Studies*, January 1997, 95–143.

83. A report on this event is archived at http://www-tech.mit.edu/archives/VOL_089/TECH_V089_S0117_P005.txt.

84. B. Russell (1912), *The Problems of Philosophy*. Oxford: Oxford University Press.

85. R. Dawkins (2006), *The God Delusion*. New York: Houghton-Mifflin.

86. Ibid.

87. The story of the 'Ring of Gyges' is presented in Book II of the *Republic*. See Plato (1979), *The Republic* (trans. R. Larson). Arlington Heights, IL: Harlan Davidson.

88. J. Sartre (1957), *Existentialism and Human Emotions*. New York: Philosophical Library.

89. B. Schwartz (2004), 'The Tyranny of Choice'. *Scientific American*, http://www.sciam.com/article.cfm?chanID=sa006&colID=1&articleID=0006AD38-D9FB-1055-973683414B7F0000.

90. A. Long and D. Sedley (1987), *The Hellenistic Philosophers*. Cambridge: Cambridge University Press.

91. J. Minkel (2002), 'Reality Check'. *Scientific American*, http://www.sciam.com/article.cfm?articleID=00064803-8072-1D9B-815A809EC5880000&sc=I100322.

92. Nicholas H. Steneck has written extensively on this subject. See his 'Research Integrity and Scientific Misconduct' in *Higher Education in the United States: An Encyclopedia*, edited by James F. Forest and Kevin Kinser (Santa Barbara, CA: ABC-CLIO, 2002); 'Research Ethics and Regulation' in *Higher Education in the United States: An Encyclopedia*; 'Research Misconduct' in *Encyclopedia of Education* (New York: MacMillan, 2002); 'Institutional and Individual Responsibilities for Integrity in Research' in *American Journal of Bioethics* 2 (4) (2002), 51–3; *Investigating Research Integrity: Proceedings of the First ORI Research Conference on Research Integrity* (Washington, DC: Office of Research Integrity, 2002); and 'Confronting Misconduct in Science in the 1980s and 1990s: What Has and Has Not Been Accomplished?' in *Science and Engineering Ethics* 5 (2) (1999): 161–76.

93. T. Hobbes (1962), *Leviathan*. New York: Collier Books.

94. R. Dawkins (1986), *The Blind Watchmaker*. New York: W. W. Norton & Company.

95. This view of morality is presented in the 'Ring of Gyges' in Book II of the *Republic*. See Plato (1979), *The Republic* (trans. R. Larson). Arlington Heights, IL: Harlan Davidson.

96. T. Hobbes (1962), *Leviathan*. New York: Collier Books.

97. See, for example, http://news.bbc.co.uk/1/hi/technology/4645596.stm. See also C. Thomson (2006), 'Google's China Problem (and China's Google Problem)'. *The New York Times*, http://www.nytimes.com/2006/04/23/magazine/23google.html?ex=1303444800&en=972002761056363f&ei=5090.

98. T. Zeller (2006), 'House Member Criticizes Internet Companies for Practices in China'. *The New York Times*, http://www.nytimes.com/2006/02/15/technology/15cnd-Internet.html?ex=1297659600&en=1d2dce56f6c4a728&ei=5088&partner=rssnyt&emc=rss.

99. The story, in the *St Petersburg Times*, can be read at http://www.sptimes.com/2007/01/30/State/Judge__2_years_each_f.shtml.

100. *Wired* magazine was quick to discuss this matter. See M. Delio (2002), 'The Dark Side of Hacking Bill'. *Wired*, http://www.wired.com/politics/law/news/2002/07/54153.

101. Locke presents his view of the state of nature in Book II, Chapter II of his *Treatise*. See Locke (1952), *The Second Treatise of Government*. New York: Bobbs-Merrill.

102. A transcript of a CNN interview in which he defends torture is located at http://edition.cnn.com/2003/LAW/03/03/cnna.Dershowitz/.

103. Torture is extensively discussed in E. Thomas and M. Hirsh (2005), 'The Debate over Torture'. *Newsweek*, http://www.msnbc.msn.com/id/10020629/site/newsweek/.

104. A. Mcoy (2006), 'The Myth of the Ticking Time Bomb'. *The Progressive*, http://www.progressive.org/mag_mccoy1006.

105. The transcript of her conversation with Crossfire's Tucker Carlson is on CNN.com: http://www.cnn.com/2003/SHOWBIZ/Music/09/03/cnna.spears/.

106. This is discussed in Chapter VIII of the *Second Treatise*. See J. Locke (1952), *The Second Treatise of Government*. New York: Bobbs-Merrill.

107. See the Institute's information at http://www.iom.edu/?id=19175. See also L. Gnagey (2004), 'Institute of Medicine Calls for Universal Health

Insurance'. *The University Record Online*, http://www.umich.edu/
~urecord/0304/Jan19_04/00.shtml.

108. G. Cowley (2005), 'Chasing Black Fever'. *Newsweek*, http://www.msnbc.
msn.com/id/8715762/site/newsweek/. Additional data on this disease
is available at http://www.medicalnewstoday.com/medicalnews.php?
newsid=22862 and http://www.oneworldhealth.org/pdf/Leishmaniasis
%20Fact%20Sheet.pdf?PHPSESSID=273cf3518b45b20487046a37112
7f400.

109. This challenge is presented in Book II of the *Republic*. Plato (1979), *The
Republic* (trans. R. Larson). Arlington Heights, IL: Harlan Davidson.

110. J. Alter (2005), 'The Real Price of Propaganda'. *Newsweek*. http://www.
msnbc.msn.com/id/10313724/site/newsweek/.

Bibliography

Ackerman, J. (2002), 'Food: How Safe?'. *National Geographic*, May, 2–50.

Adler, J. (2007), 'Decoding "The Secret"'. *Newsweek*, http://www.msnbc.msn.com/id/17314883/site/newsweek/.

Adler, J. and T. Weingarten (2005), 'The Flap over Foie Gras'. *Newsweek*, 2 May, 58.

Alter, J. (2005), 'Monkey See, Monkey Do'. *Newsweek*, 15 August, 27.

Alter, J. (2005), 'The Real Price of Propaganda'. *Newsweek*, http://www.msnbc.msn.com/id/10313724/site/newsweek/.

Armstrong, A. (1989), *Universals*. Westview, CO: Boulder.

Aristotle (1991), *The Complete Works of Aristotle* (two vols) (ed. J. Barnes). Princeton, NJ: Princeton University Press.

Bloom, P. (2004), *Descartes' Baby: How the Science of Child Development Explains What Makes Us Human*. New York: Basic Books.

Blume, D. (1993), 'Getting Tough on College Sports'. *Chronicle of Higher Education*, http://chronicle.com/che-data/articles.dir/articles-40.dir/issue-04.dir/04a03901.htm.

Borland, J. (2002), 'ISP Download Caps to Slow Swapping?'. *News.com*, http://news.com.com/2100-1023-975320.html.

Brizendine, L. (2006), *The Female Brain* (1st edn). New York: Morgan Road Books.

Byrne, R. (2006), *The Secret*. New York: Beyond Words Publishing.

Campbell, K. (1990), *Abstract Particulars*. Cambridge: Basil Blackwell.

Carey, B. (2006), 'A Shocker: Partisan Thought is Unconscious'. *New York Times*, http://www.nytimes.com/2006/01/24/science/24find.html?ex=1177819200&en=7f01162b58b02786&ei=5070.

Cowley, G. (2005), 'Chasing Black Fever'. *Newsweek*, http://www.msnbc.msn.com/id/8715762/site/newsweek/.

Darnovsky, M. (2004), 'Revisiting Sex Selection: The Growing Popularity of New Sex Selection Methods Revives an Old Debate'. *Council for Responsible Genetics*, http://www.gene-watch.org/genewatch/articles/17-1darnovsky.html.

Dawkins, R. (1986), *The Blind Watchmaker*. New York: W. W. Norton & Company.

Dawkins, R. (2006), *The God Delusion*. New York: Houghton-Mifflin.

Delio, M. (2002), 'The Dark Side of Hacking Bill'. *Wired*, http://www.wired.com/politics/law/news/2002/07/54153.

Descartes, R. (1988), *The Philosophical Writings of Descartes: Volume I* (trans. J. Cottingham, R. Stoothoff and D. Murdoch). Avon: Cambridge University Press.

Descartes, R. (1988), *The Philosophical Writings of Descartes: Volume II* (trans. J. Cottingham, R. Stoothoff and D. Murdoch). Avon: Cambridge University Press.

Edgers, G. (2003), 'Sculptor Sues Fidelity to Keep his Artistic Vision Intact'. *Boston Globe*, http://www.boston.com/ae/theater_arts/articles/2003/10/07/sculptor_sues_fidelity_to_keep_his_artistic_vision_intact/.

Flam, B. (2006), 'One Big STEP: Another Major Study Confirms that Distant Prayers Do Not Heal the Sick'. *Skeptical Inquirer*, July/August 2006, 5–6.

Frey, J. (2003), *A Million Little Pieces*. New York: Random House.

Gavora, J. (2002), *Tilting the Playing Field*. San Francisco, CA: Encounter Books.

Gnagey, L. (2004), 'Institute of Medicine Calls for Universal Health Insurance'. *The University Record Online*, http://www.umich.edu/~urecord/0304/Jan19_04/00.shtml.

Graham, S. (2001), 'Parkinson's Patients Feel the Placebo Effect'. *Scientific America*, http://www.sciam.com/article.cfm?articleID=000A97F8-9525-1C60-B882809EC588ED9F.

Graham, S. (2004), 'Scientists See How Placebo Effect Eases Pain'. *Scientific America*, http://www.sciam.com/article.cfm?articleID=000B6140-F61E-1034-B61E83414B7F0000&sc=I100322.

Handelman, S. (2007), 'The Memory Hacker'. *Popular Science*, 27 April, 66.

Hanley, C. (2006), 'Poll: Half of America Still Believes in WMD'. *Bangor Daily News*, 7 August, A5.

Hansmann, H. and M. Santilli (1997), 'Authors' and Artists' Moral Rights: A Comparative Legal and Economic Analysis'. *The Journal of Legal Studies*, January, 95–143.

Hays, K. (2003), 'Cloned Cat isn't a Carbon Copy', http://www.cbsnews.com/stories/2003/01/21/tech/main537380.shtml.

Hobbes, T. (1962), *Leviathan*. New York: Collier Books.

Hoffman, H. (2004), 'Virtual Reality Therapy', *Scientific America*, August, 58–65.

Hume, D. (1989), *A Treatise of Human Nature* (2nd edn) (ed. P. Nidditch). Oxford: Oxford University Press.

Irwin, M. (2006), 'Rated V for Violence'. *PC Magazine*, 7 March, 152–3.

Kant, I. (1965), *Critique of Pure Reason* (trans. J. Ellington), New York: St Martin's Press.

Kant, I. (1977), *Prolegomena to Any Future Metaphysics* (trans. P. Carus, rev. with intro. by James Ellington). Indianapolis, IN: Hackett Publishers.

Kluger, J. (1997), 'Will We Follow the Sheep?'. *Time*, http://www.time.com/time/magazine/article/0,9171,986024-2,00.html.

Lewin, T. (2006), 'At Colleges, Women are Leaving Men in the Dust'. *The New York Times*, http://www.nytimes.com/2006/07/09/education/09college.html?ex=1310097600&en=cd9efba2e9595dec&ei=5088&partner=rssnyt&emc=rss.

Locke, J. (1975), *An Essay Concerning Human Understanding* (ed. P. Nidditch). Oxford: Oxford University Press.

Locke, J. (1952), *The Second Treatise of Government*. New York: Bobbs-Merrill.

Long, A. and D. Sedley (1987), *The Hellenistic Philosophers*. Cambridge: Cambridge University Press.

Mcoy, A. (2006), 'The Myth of the Ticking Time Bomb', *The Progressive*, http://www.progressive.org/mag_mccoy1006.

Minkel, J. (2002), 'Reality Check'. *Scientific American*, http://www.sciam.com/article.cfm?articleID=00064803-8072-1D9B-815A809EC5880000 &sc=I100322.

Mosley J., K. O'Malley, N. Petersen, T. Menke, B. Brody, D. Kuykendall, J. Hollingsworth, C. Ashton and N. Wray (2002), 'A Controlled Trial of Arthroscopic Surgery for Osteoarthritis of the Knee', *The New England Journal of Medicine*, http://content.nejm.org/cgi/content/abstract/347/2/81.

Newman, S. (2001), 'Australian Mouse Study Confirms CRG Warning', http://www.gene-watch.org/genewatch/articles/14-2mousestuart.html.

Occam (1957), *Philosophical Writings* (ed. and trans. P. Boehner). Edinburgh: Nelson.

Peyser, M. (2006), 'The Ugly Truth'. *Newsweek*, 23 January, 62–4.

Plato (1889), *The Dialogues of Plato* (trans. B. Jowett). New York: Scribner's.

Plato (1896), *The Dialogues of Plato* (3rd edn) (trans. B. Jowett). Oxford: Oxford University Press.

Plato (1941), *The Republic of Plato* (trans. F. Cornford). London: Oxford University Press.

Plato (1979), *The Republic* (trans. R. Larson). Arlington Heights, IL: Harlan Davidson.

Plato (1981), *Five Dialogies: Euthyphro, Apology, Crito, Meno, Phaedo* (trans. G. Grube). Indianapolis, IN: Hacket Publishing Company, Inc.

Rennie, J. (2002), '15 Answers to Creationist Nonsense'. *Scientific America*, July, 78–85.

Russell, B. (1912), *The Problems of Philosophy*. Oxford: Oxford University Press.

Sartre, J. (1957), *Existentialism and Human Emotions*. New York: Philosophical Library.

Scelfo, J. (2005), 'Bad Girls Go Wild'. *Newsweek*, 13 June, 66–7

Scelfo, J. and P. Tyre (2006), 'Why Girls Will Be Girls'. *Newsweek*, 31 July, 46–7.

Somers, C. (2000), *The War against Boys – How Misguided Feminism is Harming our Young Men*. New York: Simon & Shuster.

Springen, K. (2006), 'This is Your Brain on Alien Killer Pimps of Nazi Doom'. *Newsweek*, 11 December, 48.

Schwartz, B. (2004, 'The Tyranny of Choice'. *Scientific American*, http://www.sciam.com/article.cfm?chanID=sa006&colID=1&articleID=0006AD38-D9FB-1055-973683414B7F0000.

Steneck, H. (2002), 'Research Integrity and Scientific Misconduct'. In *Higher Education in the United States: An Encyclopedia* (ed. James F. Forest and Kevin Kinser). Santa Barbara, CA: ABC-CLIO.

Steneck, H. (2002), 'Research Ethics and Regulation'. In *Higher Education in the United States: An Encyclopedia* (ed. by James F. Forest and Kevin Kinser). Santa Barbara, CA: ABC-CLIO.

Steneck, H. (2002), 'Research Misconduct'. In *Encyclopedia of Education*. New York: MacMillan.

Steneck, H. (2002), 'Institutional and Individual Responsibilities for Integrity in Research'. *American Journal of Bioethics* 2 (4), 51–3.

Steneck, H. (2002), *Investigating Research Integrity: Proceedings of the First ORI Research Conference on Research Integrity*. Washington, DC: Office of Research Integrity.

Steneck, H. (1999), 'Confronting Misconduct in Science in the 1980s and 1990s: What Has and Has Not Been Accomplished?'. *Science and Engineering Ethics* 5 (2), 161–76.

Thomas, E. and M. Hirsh (2005), 'The Debate over Torture'. *Newsweek*, http://www.msnbc.msn.com/id/10020629/site/newsweek/.

Thomson, C. (2006), 'Google's China Problem (and China's Google Problem)', *The New York Times*, http://www.nytimes.com/2006/04/23/magazine/23google.html?ex=1303444800&en=972002761056363f&ei=5090.

Tyre, P. (2005), 'Boy Brains, Girl Brains'. *Newsweek*, 19 September, 59.

Zeller, T. (2006), 'House Member Criticizes Internet Companies for Practices in China', *The New York Times*, http://www.nytimes.com/2006/02/15/technology/15cnd-Internet.html?ex=1297659600&en=1d2dce56f6c4a728&ei=5088&partner=rssnyt&emc=rss.

Index